TWO YEARS IN THE MELTING POT

by
LIU ZONGREN

Introduction by Linda Yu

CHINA
BOOKS
& Periodicals, Inc.

San Francisco

Chapter titles designed in Chinese calligraphic script by well-known Chinese artist Tang You Shan

Cover and book design by Sharon Smith

First edition, 1984

Library of Congress Catalog Card Number: 84-12090
ISBN 0-8351-1370-1 (paperback)
ISBN 0-8351-1371-X (casebound)

Printed in the United States of America by

CHINA BOOKS
& Periodicals, Inc.
2929 24th Street,
San Francisco CA 94110

CONTENTS

INTRODUCTION

"Do the Chinese always eat so much at every meal?"
It was the fifth day in China, and the native-born
Americans in the group kept asking questions that,
to my way of thinking, were becoming more and
more irritating.

How little they understood simple hospitality, I
thought to myself. The "foreign friends," as the Chinese called all tourists, were being fed three huge
meals each day in the tour. Whether it was a hotel
breakfast (choice of Chinese or American), lunch or
dinner at local restaurants, the tables were piled high
with plates of food, always representative of the province we were visiting.

I had spent 30 of the 35 years of my life in America
...but since I was on a return trip to the land of my
birth, and since I still spoke enough Chinese to inter-
pret for the other travellers, I had become the
unofficial source of explanations on the mysteries of
the East.

I bit my tongue, opting for Chinese patience and
tried to explain that, of course, all Chinese could not
yet eat this well. Some mouths were undoubtedly going unfilled so that visitors could enjoy China with full
bellies. I further explained that centuries of Chinese
custom, politeness, and hospitality required that
guests eat their fill before hosts would venture to
taste. What I did not add was that I supposed the
Chinese took one look at the much larger size of the
"foreign friends" and immediately calculated it would
indeed take huge amounts of food to satisfy their ap-

petites. And so I was introduced to the chasm between American and Chinese culture.

It wasn't many days later that I walked to the other side of the chasm. One morning, I pulled on some clean clothes, a commodity in relatively short supply when covering a Chinese city every two days. A friend and I decided to stop in Shanghai's largest department store. We had been assured this cosmopolitan store in China's most modern city would treat us like Saturday morning customers at Marshall Fields. Walking through the store, it was uncomfortably apparent that we were not blending in with the crowd. It was not possible to lose track of me, my friend said later, since streams of people formed a parade behind me, tracing my every step. The red jeans I so nonchalantly put on a few hours before created havoc at Shanghai's #10 Department Store. When I paused to pay attention, I heard shocked voices wonder at the brazenness of this Chinese woman, venturing so shamelessly through the crowded store, decked out in bright, attention garnering red.

With these experiences behind me, I approached Liu Zongren's book with excitement. He, as a practicing Chinese journalist, will teach me something, I thought, as he looks with quizzical eye at the things we take for granted; with shocked amazement at the things we accept as normal; and with amusement at the things that make us proud. And, I hoped, with a universal understanding of man's weaknesses when he saw the things that are tragic in our society. I have found some of all those things in this journal.

But I found more. I found the story of a man of courage. It may not occur to many of us to consider how lonely life might be in another country, separated from spouse and child, home, co-workers, friends, and all that is familiar. Homesickness and the barriers created by new foods, climate, and language might justifiably be dealt with by a more and more reclusive attitude. But one of the Americans Liu wrote about in his journal described him this way.

"I remember him as a gentle person, reserved, coupled with an openness and vulnerability," says Meg Moritz, a television producer in Chicago. "He changed during his stay here from being something of a stranger in a strange land to someone who seemed very comfortable and accepting of American ways. I think what I saw in him was an ability to open up to people and to a culture that must have at first seemed very alien."

And how alien we truly are! It is a delight to see ourselves through the eyes of this man of China. Did it ever occur to us that our values might be misplaced when we are willing to "spend $100 on a metal detector that is used to find pennies"? Or that we will wear ourselves out jogging an hour each day to maintain weight, but "will usually drive to work over a distance they could cover in twenty minutes by walking."

Not all of Liu's observations about us are such pleasant lessons. He has some disturbing stories to tell about how he discovered racism and segregation in our society, and how he found out about crime.

Despite fluctuations in the gauge of government to government relations, the official Chinese policy seems to reflect a genuine feeling among China's people of near universal affection for Americans. An American visitor to China finds friendly words, helpful attitudes, and special treatment everywhere.

But Liu was sent to a country which has long been a melting pot. We have accepted so many people, ideas, languages, and customs that many of us do not welcome more. There is no public policy that causes Americans to reach out in friendship to foreign friends. And more than that, many of us are not even aware of their presence among us.

Liu's Chicago journalist friend, Ron Dorfman, puts it well in speaking of writers who have observed the United States. "Foreigners are able to look at us with a cooler eye." We can learn much about ourselves through the cool eyes of Liu Zongren.

And once we learn about ourselves, perhaps we will want to include in our understanding the most populous nation on earth. If we do not understand each other, how can the inquisitive Liu Zongren's of the world know why our nation would collectively mourn the violent passing of John Lennon in what he called "hero worship for a guitar player." If we do not comprehend each other's ways, how can the Liu Zongren's of the world explain how hundreds of thousands of Chinese could be caught up once in frenzied chanting of slogans from Chairman Mao's *Little Red Book*.

There is a long way to go before the Chinese and American people can change enough to learn about and understand one another. I like the way one Chinese friend said it: It takes wave after wave to make a dent in the shore.

I hope the understanding you develop from *Two Years in the Melting Pot* will begin a tidal wave.

by Linda Yu,
television reporter for WLS-TV
(Channel 7) Chicago

CHAPTER ONE

THOUGHTS ABOVE THE CLOUDS

It was a cold, late-November day in 1980. I had allowed only my wife, Fengyun, and my son, Ze, to bring me to the airport and see me off. I was about to leave Beijing, China to study in the United States on a two-year fellowship. In a country that has very little currency to spend on scholars traveling abroad, I was fortunate to be one of the very few selected.

We arrived promptly at 11:00 P.M., and after checking in we found that many of the forty-six visiting scholars, bound for many different U.S. universities, were already there. Fengyun looked sad and my heart ached. I wanted to take her in my arms and tell her how much I would miss her, but that is not the Chinese custom. She is a strong-willed person who had been keeping her emotions in check for a long time, but today I saw her eyes shimmering. Although we really hadn't said much to each other in the past several days, we now seemed to have exhausted all words. What could I say to her? She fussed with my travel bag and scolded me: "Don't lose your things—you always forget something. The woolen underwear is at the bottom of your case. Put it on when you get there. They say Chicago is very cold."

For the past half month I had been so wrapped up in my own problems and preparations that, in the last days, she complained about my neglecting her—I should not have squeezed onto the bus the way I did the other day; I should have given her more love and comfort. Now I wanted to apologize and tell her I understood. I looked at her face. She was thirty-four this year, a beautiful woman I had known for fifteen years. Now her skin was not so smooth anymore. How time flies. And in all of those years, with all that had happened, how few happy periods we had had together. Now we were to be separated, again.

I heard a woman sob. She was the wife of one of the others from our group. I wished Fengyun could weep; I had never seen her cry in public, but I always knew when she felt pain. Ze, our eleven-year-old son, was excited to be in this grand airport for the first time, but he seemed to sense what was happening. He took Fengyun's hand and said to me, "Write to us when you arrive in the United States."

"Ze, you are old enough to help your mother," I said.

"Yes," he smiled, still such a young child.

I turned to my wife. "Take care of yourself, Fengyun. We'll make up for our loss when I come home."

I hurried to catch up with the others. When I turned to look back, I saw Fengyun weeping. Even when I was taken away in 1973 for a two year stay in a labor reformation center, during the Cultural Revolution, she hadn't shed a tear.

As I walked toward the plane I wondered if this journey would be worth the sacrifice to my personal life. When I had confessed to friends that I was not enthusiastic about going away, some didn't believe me. They thought I was pretending to be modest, and Fengyun warned me not to say such silly things. It was a paradox. On the one hand, I had been eager to win this chance, which would give me

2

two years to look at a foreign country and would enhance my reputation. I often felt that others in the office of *China Reconstructs*, where I worked as an English translator, looked down on my abilities because I had never gone to college. This would rectify that situation. But on the other hand, I hated to leave my family, as I had been forced to do just a few years before. By nature I was a homebody; I disliked traveling, even inside China. For these others, who were walking now beside me onto the plane, study abroad might be a joy, a free vacation trip. For me, it would only be an opportunity to improve my professional skills.

When we boarded the giant 747 C.A.A.C. plane, the stewardess told us that we could use the empty seats for napping. The rear part of the plane was mostly empty. I settled into a seat and looked around. Out of this twenty-third group of scholars going abroad, all but a few of us were over forty years of age; only four were women; only one had been abroad before. As they talked animatedly among themselves, I envied their cheerfulness. I could not forget the sad expression on Fengyun's face. We fastened our seat belts and the plane moved into position for lift off. I pressed my face against the window of the plane as we rose into the air, straining to see the last lights of Beijing.

This was my first trip abroad and my first time in one of these gigantic planes. I had expected to feel excitement and curiosity, but felt neither. The cabin felt too warm. Since it was late fall, I, like most Beijing residents, was wearing a woolen sweater and woolen underwear to protect me from the cold weather. I decided to go into the washroom and take them off. I hoped that the clothes I had brought along would be suitable for America. At the end of the four-day orientation, we were told that we had only forty days in which to prepare to leave. Each of the eighty-six people, going to eight different countries, was issued 700 yuan (the equivalent of 400 U.S. dollars) and an official letter that

3

allowed us to enter a special clothing store and a special tailor shop. In a country where people spend 70 to 80 percent of their incomes on food, we needed such a subsidy in order to buy extra clothes before we went abroad. Fengyun accompanied me on all the shopping trips. Ron Dorfman went with us to the tailor shop. Ron, a journalist from Chicago, working at that time for *China Reconstructs* on a one-year contract, had become my friend after five months in my office. He had also offered to help me find a university in the Chicago area. The tailor we went to served only foreign diplomats and residents, and a few privileged Chinese. Since Ron, an American expert, was with me, I was taken more seriously by the tailor who measured me. I chose a suit in Chinese style of good quality material, thinking that, after two years, I would be able to wear it for special occasions. I also bought a less expensive western-style suit, knowing that I wouldn't have much use for it after I returned to China. I didn't need the entire 700 yuan. I took most of my old clothes with me, packing them in a 4 x 2 1/2-foot canvas suitcase that I bought at a discount counter in Beijing for 18 yuan.

The lights were dim in the plane now and I wanted to sleep through all the unpleasant thoughts about leaving home, but I couldn't. I should have felt exalted being on my way to the United States. In that country I could improve my journalistic skills, learn much about the world and experience another culture. During all of my forty years I had been fighting to improve myself. In school I read classical Chinese literature and dreamed of becoming a writer. I played soccer, attended swimming and skating classes at the Beijing Children's Palace, and learned to play the violin from a young man in our courtyard. I also practiced martial arts at a private school. Sad to say, I never became a master of music, sports or anything else. I found myself sticking with one thing only long enough to understand what it was all about.

4

My job with *China Reconstructs* was challenging because the magazine carried a range of subjects that provided new knowledge every day. My only dissatisfaction while working there was my lack of a college diploma. Now I was bound for a country which might eventually afford even more than a diploma. But I would be six thousand miles away, on the other side of the earth, away from Fengyun. My thoughts kept drifting longingly back to her.

• • •

I first met Fengyun in March 1965. I had just returned from the army and was staying with my mother for two weeks. Soon I would be attending the Foreign Languages Bureau Training School, and I was having a wonderful time parading around in my new civilian clothes, conscious of my youth and my spirit, and fully prepared to take on the new challenge.

The day before registration, I took a bus to the school, located in Fragrance Hill Park in the western suburb of Beijing. Fengyun was in the registration office, sitting solemnly at a desk, taking down the names of newcomers. Later I learned she had come to the school directly from the army unit in which she had served for three years as a telegraph operator. She was still wearing her faded, winter army uniform, her short hair held in place by a piece of red woolen cord. She looked like a serious young country girl, and I was attracted to her from the beginning.

Fengyun and I were assigned to the same English language class, and she was one of only two women among forty-five students. She sat alone practicing pronunciation for hours after class and, in the evening, she always walked by herself back to the dormitory. One night I caught up with her walking along the deserted, dimly lit, mile-long path to the dorm. When she didn't appear surprised at my boldness, I knew she was a brave woman.

We were silent most of the way, but I felt myself strangely drawn to her. Her mother had died when she was nine and since she was not on good terms with her stepmother, she didn't really have a family in Beijing. From then on, I worried when she didn't return to her room by 9:00 P.M. And I scolded her as if she were a child for not eating breakfast (to save time, she would eat cold steamed bread from the night before). By the time the Cultural Revolution started in August 1966, we were so close to each other that our classmates had stopped talking about our constantly being together, assuming we were going to marry.

We were married in November 1968. In December, she was assigned to be a librarian at the Foreign Languages Publishing Bureau and I started working for *China Reconstructs*. Our offices were in the same building. We went to and from work together. During the next fourteen years we were to separate only twice: once when she worked for a year on a farm in a re-education program for office workers, and again during the two years I spent in the labor reformation center.

We had our disagreements, and there were times when we didn't like one another very much. Sometimes I thought life might be better for both of us if we were alone; we could then invest all of our time and energy in our careers. But this notion disappeared whenever I was away from her. While she was living on the farm, our home didn't hold any attraction for me, and I didn't know what to do after work. I didn't know where I should have my supper—whether I should eat at the office canteen, cook at home, or buy a pancake at a restaurant. Often I just had a dish of cold meat and a glass of wine.

On Saturday afternoons I would fetch my four-year-old son from the kindergarten where he stayed five and a half days a week. The two of us would spend the rest of the day in a restaurant or in a park, but it was never the same as it was when there were the three of us. Fengyun made us a family.

Even more difficult was our second separation. I will

never forget the day in 1975 when I was released from the labor reformation center. After two years of counting the days, I felt no excitement about seeing my family, no anxiety—almost no thoughts whatsoever. The anger and the hatred of the past were gone. I had only my mental picture of Fengyun and Ze. The thought of them had made my heart ache. I swore then that I would make it up to her and never leave her again. She would not suffer anymore. Yet, here I was in this plane, looking out at the moon shining down on the clouds, carried again by my ambitions, involved in another unpredictable struggle.

For the past fifteen years I had had too many ups and downs. If I hadn't been ambitious, perhaps I wouldn't have found myself in the labor reformation center, perhaps I wouldn't have had so much cause to suffer. I had tried to tell myself to be content with an uneventful life. No one else in my family had ever committed crimes or been involved with the police. My grandfather, an illiterate peasant in a prosperous village on the outskirts of Tangshan, an industrial city northeast of Beijing, never allowed his fourteen children even to use an indecent word. He sent his three sons and youngest daughter to school. He was thirty-nine when my father, the eldest, left home to apprentice in a construction company. My father later became an architect, proud that he was a self-made man. I lived in the village until age ten, going to the same school as my father. I loved those years, swimming in the pond behind our backyard, stealing grapes from the vines in the front yard, catching crickets in the cornfields.

My father found a permanent job in Beijing in 1950 and brought the family to the city. Fully occupied with his work, he paid little attention to my schooling. I was delayed three years in graduating from grade school because, as the eldest child, I had to share my mother's burden of looking after my three younger brothers and baby sister. Even so, I read in the evenings and I never failed to rate highest in my classes. I finished junior high school at the age of eighteen.

My family wanted me to go to high school, but I was impatient and desired an easier path to a career. In 1959 I joined the army. My father found out about my decision the night before I was to leave, when he returned from Burma where he was building a textile mill. I came home from a movie to find him sitting in a chair, still in his traveling clothes. He looked unhappy; my mother was silent. I didn't know what to say. He told me not to forget my textbooks, to study by myself so that I could go to college later.

During those six years in the service, I managed to finish college mathematics and geometry and to spend endless hours studying Chinese literature. In February 1965, when I was discharged, the Foreign Languages Publishing Bureau in Beijing sent representatives out to select veterans to be trained in foreign languages. I was selected and enrolled and I thought that this, perhaps, would be my future.

I spent twelve hours a day learning English, but at the end of one year, China's schools were closed when the Cultural Revolution began. My school closed when a few zealous students demanded that classes end, and the administration was more than ready to leave the sensitive political situation to the students. Teachers, foreign and Chinese, stopped coming. Most students became "full-time revolutionaries," attacking old traditions, social norms—anything old. Then they attacked old people, beating up landowners, former owners of businesses, and officials of the old regime. Agitated by people in high places, they began attacking any government officials who were in disagreement with the Cultural Revolution. Finally, the young people fought among themselves for the title of "most revolutionary." I was then almost thirty and I bitterly resented this interruption; how much time would I have left to learn a profession? While others were making revolution, I stayed in my dormitory studying my English books.

A year later, in 1968, I was given a job at *China Recon-*

structs, a Chinese magazine published in six languages. The magazine was designed to introduce Chinese culture, arts and current events to the outside world. With my lack of education, I was ill-equipped to function in the world of international publishing. I started as a proofreader, then I typed manuscripts. My colleagues in the office, three Americans and four Chinese, all educated in the United States, were better English teachers than those in my school. My ambition was to surpass my colleagues within ten years. I stuck to my job and, outside of work, I read many English books.

In 1970, several of my former schoolmates who now also worked for the magazine were accused of criminal activities. Their only fault, as radicals in the early days of the revolution, was being overzealous in following the instructions of their leaders, who had now fallen from grace. I had avoided any involvement in factional fighting during that 1966-1969 period of turmoil, and was too naive in my thinking that none of this involved me. A stupid argument with a senior bureau official over the activities of my colleagues landed me in the detention room of the office building. For a month and a half I was confined, interrogated, and criticized at mass meetings. Out of fear, I wrote a confession, accusing myself of reactionary ideas. But I felt wronged; I wept and appealed to the authorities, claiming my innocence. They wouldn't listen, only saying that since I was protecting counter-revolutionaries, I was also a counter revolutionary.

My bitterness grew. Eventually I was released from confinement and assigned to the office kitchen as a laborer. I chopped wood and cleaned the dining hall. My humiliation and frustration grew into anger and I protested loudly and openly, accusing the authorities of being fascists. The consequence was a sentence of two years in the labor reformation center, in a remote location three hundred miles from Beijing.

The center was composed of leaky, crumbling one-story barracks built by the new Chinese government in the early 1950s, used to incarcerate the old regime's officials, secret agents and hooligans. Our courtyard, holding 150 men, was in a compound surrounded by high walls. Most of us in this courtyard were people whose crimes were not serious enough to come before a court, but serious enough for us to be separated from the public.

At night I slept on a large brick platform along with thieves, pickpockets, rapists and homosexuals. The one bare light bulb which burned all night gave off just enough light to allow me to read. I read everything I could get my hands on—in Chinese or English—still confident that someday I could become a good translator. In summer, I sweated through the hot days in steamy rice fields. In winter, I watched my numb fingers turn red, then white, while digging through frozen top soil to make ditches.

My sentence was reduced by six months, for good behavior. But those 714 days and nights of imprisonment were the longest in my life so far. On the day of my leaving, I had packed my things early in the morning, put them on a cart, and waited in the courtyard for the official on duty to hand me my release papers. It was a warm Sunday with a blue sky and bright sun. The inmates were outside, some washing clothes at the single tap, some playing cards.

Close to noon, an officer came with the paper that meant my freedom. A guard on a horse-drawn cart took me the three miles to the railway station. Along the way we bumped over deep ruts formed during rainy days, then dried hard by the sun. Over this road Fengyun had traveled dozens of times, often by foot, dragging our four-year-old son along, to bring me dried beef, canned meat and chicken. She worried that the camp food was not nutritious. We finally arrived at the empty station and the driver helped me carry my luggage to the platform. When I bought my ticket, the passengers—security officers and

10

their families, and released camp inmates—looked at me knowingly. They were the only other people who used this station. I boarded the train, ignoring their curious gazes; I had nothing to be ashamed of.

• • •

The first sunshine of the next morning aboard the plane revealed snow-capped mountains and the blue waters of the Mediterranean. Everyone was awakening, talking in whispers, as the stewardesses brought our breakfast. What were the histories of these other travelers—why were they leaving China? Had they also spent difficult lives in preparation for this journey?

I had had no idea that I would be able to become a scholar and travel when I returned to my job at *China Reconstructs*, after being in prison. Still in disgrace, avoided by my colleagues, I was not allowed to take part in their long political meetings and discussions, their readings of government documents. It suited me fine to be left alone to engage in "self-study of political materials." Reading English was regarded as neglecting one's political education, a very serious offense, but the English books on the office shelves were too tempting. I learned to quickly substitute Mao's works for *David Copperfield* when others came around.

In November 1975, Premier Zhou Enlai died. The continuing rumors about Chairman Mao Zedong's ill health fired public unrest. Then, in Sept. 1976, Chairman Mao died. Nobody believed Jiang Qing (Chairman Mao's widow) and her followers could stay in power for long. In a quick sweep, the old hands in the Chinese Communist Party arrested Jiang Qing and her close associates. Deng Xiaoping was returned to leadership and given a free hand. First, he restored to the leading positions the old party leaders who had been purged during the Cultural Revolution. Those persecuted for political disagreement were exonerated. In October 1978, after eight years of disgrace, my name was cleared.

I plunged into my work, taking on more responsibility for major articles. Then in May 1980, I took the government examination for the fellowship. The three candidates with the best command of English would be allowed to study abroad for two years at the expense of the Ministry of Education. Most of the twenty applicants had graduated from college before 1965, the year I began my study of English, and yet I came out on top in the examination. Many people urged me to go to the United States.

It was then that Ron Dorfman made a phone call for me from Beijing to the dean of the Medill School of Journalism at Northwestern University in Evanston, Illinois. Ten days later I received, from Northwestern, Form IAP-66, the key document for exchange of visiting scholars between China and the United States.

● ● ●

It was midday and I was tired from this long journey as we began the final part of our flight, across the Atlantic Ocean, to land at Washington, D.C. How would I be treated in America? How would I feel being alone there? At the orientation, a Chinese diplomat briefed us on how to behave at a dinner table, how to use silverware and how to dress. A vice-minister encouraged us to study hard for the cause of building socialist China and for the country's modernization. I am basically a proud person and a conservative Chinese. I have a tendency to keep my distance from certain colleagues I don't like. I was disturbed by the idea that I might be expected to respond humbly to others. In the U.S. I would have to relate to Americans, whether I liked it or not, and Americans sometimes can be arrogant and aloof.

Yet, there I was, about to realize one of my greatest ambitions, to study and live in America. But where was the elation I should be feeling?

I remembered a line from a poem I once wrote about my youth: "My thoughts fly above the clouds. My ambition rides with the wind."

CHAPTER TWO

HERE I AM A STRANGER

After a flight of twenty-two hours, we crossed over the coast of the United States and prepared for our landing at Dulles International Airport in Virginia, twenty miles west of Washington, D.C. We were all exhausted as we climbed aboard the bus which rose up to the door of the plane, then lowered and transported us into the terminal. The day was bright and clear and surrounding us was a wooded green countryside. We were met by representatives of the Chinese Embassy, who cleared us through customs and immigration, and then drove us to the embassy where we were to stay for ten days.

While the other members of our group stayed busy, taking tours and exploring the beautiful capital of the richest country in the world, I stayed alone, feeling sad and dislodged. I was suffering from jetlag and nostalgia, missing Fengyun and Ze. It was during these days that I wrote Fengyun my first letter from America:

The temperature is much the same here as in Beijing. The difference is that everywhere there is green grass. There are no crowds of people on the street. The stores are quiet and empty most of the time. I don't know how they make a living selling so little.

Our son would like this place; there are squirrels everywhere! Flocks of pigeons are fed in open lots and on sidewalks. You don't feel squeezed in as we do on Beijing streets. There is so much space. Most museums are free and in them are hundreds of TV sets showing educational programs. In the windows of stores, TVs are on all day and night. Nobody bothers to turn off the lights even during the day.

Cars and more cars—as many cars as we have bicycles. Very few people walk. There are also very few public buses. Most people drive cars, even old women drive.

At the embassy kitchen we have chicken every meal. We could have a whole chicken if we could eat it. We have apples, oranges and bananas at every meal, plenty of them. Plenty of milk. They say Americans drink milk like we drink water. But I have little appetite. This may be caused by jetlag, but I think the real reason is that I don't feel comfortable here.

During my two years in the United States, I would often wonder why I had been willing to leave Fengyun. Although it isn't unusual in modern-day China for families to be separated for long periods of time, I would continue to be amazed that I had made such a choice.

• • •

Our stay of ten days in Washington was finally over. Everyone in the group was packing, saying farewells, getting ready to be dispersed to various schools throughout the midwestern states. Up to now, various people had been responsible for all the arrangements of my trip, and had instructed me on what to do and where to go. Since this was my first time in a foreign country, I was afraid of the time when I would be on my own.

I was going to be staying in Evanston at the home of John McKnight, a professor at Northwestern University, and a friend of Ron Dorfman's. Ron had written to Professor McKnight and asked him to look after me until Ron returned to the United States for Christmas, which was still several weeks away. The embassy had notified Professor McKnight of the time of my plane's arrival at Chicago's O'Hare Airport, but what would I do if he was not there? I would have to call him. At the embassy they taught us how to use American public telephones, but I had not yet actually touched one. I hoped I would not have to call him, because it was difficult for me to understand English spoken through a telephone.

I boarded my flight to Chicago with Zheng Zhenyi, a computer science researcher, and another engineer, both of whom were going to the University of Chicago. After the flight of nearly two hours, I was greatly relieved when Professor McKnight called out my name as soon as I came off the plane and stepped through the gate. We gathered up my luggage and drove for fifty minutes on a highway to the town of Evanston. It was colder here than in Washington, the sky grey above the leafless trees. We passed through wide streets with large, handsome houses set back on lawns, with many trees and flowerbeds. At last we drove up and parked in the driveway of one of these houses, which was to be my home through the winter months.

Mrs. McKnight, a heavyset woman in her fifties, opened the door to greet me. She came forward and embraced me. I must have appeared very awkward to her when she did this; she was the first woman who had ever put her arms around me in front of others. Fengyun had never even touched my hand in public. After we exchanged a few words, Mrs. McKnight led me upstairs to my room on the second floor.

Such a huge room for one person! Rich-colored drapes

hung over the windows. A closet, a bureau, two tables and a big bed with a spring mattress. The bed sheets seemed light and silky. This would be the first time for me to sleep in such an elegant bedroom. I thought of Fengyun, how often she complained that our hard, board-bottomed bed was painful for her bad back. If at home we could have had such a bed with a spring mattress, she would surely have felt better.

I counted six lights in the room—table lights, wall lights, even a bed light. Why would one person need so many lights? At home we had only one small light in each of our two bedrooms, and we didn't turn either one on until it was needed. During my stay with the McKnights I would keep only one light on in my room, and would turn it off whenever I left the room. When the McKnights were out in the evenings, I turned off all the lights in the house except the one in the living room where I watched TV. Professor McKnight came to appreciate my frugality, and began to pay more attention to turning off the lights. He told me that his father was not rich and that those earlier times had not always been easy for him. He said that he had lived comfortably now for so long that he took for granted the luxuries the family had.

There were four members of the McKnight family. The eldest son, Scott, was away at college and the youngest son, Jonathan, was in high school. The day after I arrived, Mrs. McKnight gave me a tour of the house. Downstairs was the basement; the kitchen, living room, guest room and dining room were on the first floor; and on the second and third floors were bedrooms, half of which were unoccupied. We finished our tour back in the spacious kitchen. Mrs. McKnight opened the refrigerator, which was full of packages and bottles, and told me I was free to take out anything in it. I didn't know what the items in the refrigerator were or how to cook them, except for the eggs. In the corner of the room, she pointed out a line of bottles and said, "There is

Coke and 7-Up over there. When you are thirsty, help yourself. There's ice in the freezer. If you would like beer to drink, tell John, and he will drive you to a liquor store on Howard Street which is the dividing line between Evanston and Chicago. In Evanston the stores cannot sell alcohol."

On the kitchen table was a basket of fresh fruit, which was replenished every day. Earlier, in the basement, I had seen shelves full of different sized bottles and cans of food, and their huge freezer, solidly packed with parcels of food. I had spied some packages of big blue crabs, which I love. Mrs. McKnight had followed my gaze and taken out one of the packages for our dinner. I appreciated all that she was offering me, but I wondered: why does a family of this size need to have so much food?

She poured me a large glass of orange juice, then began preparing our lunch. I thought of my son, Ze, and of how he loves orange juice. During the summer months we would buy three or four bottles of concentrate so he could have a measured glass of it after school—but one glass only. I would urge Fengyun to drink some, but she would shake her head no, and say that it was too expensive.

Mrs. McKnight was preparing an omelette with many eggs. Eggs had been rationed for many years in Beijing— two dozen per month to a family. Fengyun, because she pays a great deal of attention to nutrition, insists that we each have one egg every day. She always took great pains to obtain eggs, buying them in the "free market" at 1.40 yuan a dozen, from peasants who brought their farm produce to the city. Sometimes friends who had connections with grocery stores also bought them for her. In this country, I found, eggs are cheap and abundant.

We had no way to store food, as I saw the McKnights do. A neighbor of ours in Beijing had once purchased a refrigerator and Fengyun had gone to see it several times. "How nice it would be to drink a cup of ice water in summer," she remarked, and I thought it would please her to have one. In the summer of 1980, I had made extra money freelancing as a translator. With this money—as much as a whole year's salary—Fengyun and I decided to buy a refrigerator. Cash in hand, we went to a store, examined several small refrigerators, but returned home empty-handed. The smallest one, with a capacity of 60 cubic liters, consumed 400 kilowatts of electricity. That would add 4 yuan to our monthly electric bill. On a salary of 56 yuan a month, this expenditure of 4 yuan cannot be taken lightly. We were already paying 1.25 yuan a month for our three lights and our nine-inch, black-and-white TV set. And, besides, we were used to buying groceries and meat every day on our way home from the office—only enough to last us until the next morning. It would not be worthwhile to spend 4 yuan just to preserve a pound of pork or to keep a bottle of water cold. Even though a bowl of cooked meat might spoil quickly in warm weather, four yuan saved on electricity would buy four pounds of pork.

The Chinese government has encouraged production of more consumer goods—color TV sets, washing machines, refrigerators—in their striving to raise the spirits of the people and modernize the country. And, although these things are in great demand, they are still very expensive.

• • •

After a few days of finally recovering from my long journey and getting used to the idea that I would be staying here, I felt a renewed loneliness for Fengyun and Ze, combined with a boredom. I didn't know anyone to visit or any place to go, or, for that matter, how to get there. My classes at the University would not begin until January 3rd, over a month away, in which there was nothing to do but wait. The big house was quiet, except for when Jonathan brought his friends home to practice their rock and roll band in the basement. I watched them sometimes, or chatted a little with Mrs. McKnight when she was home. Hanging around the house was a skill I hadn't yet mastered.

In the mornings I would wake early and watch the day begin. But I would wait to take my shower until Professor McKnight and Jonathan were finished using the bathroom next to my bedroom. Mrs. McKnight used the bathroom on the third floor. Only after the splashing sounds stopped and I was sure they were finished, would I go to take my turn in this bathroom we three shared. How nice it would be, I thought, if my family had a bathroom like this! In our small Beijing apartment the one bathroom is only large enough for a toilet and a sink for rinsing out floor mops. A larger bathroom with hot water would be wonderful, and surely if Fengyun could have a hot bath at home every day it would be good for her back. Now we can only take showers, by heating water on a gas stove and pouring it over our bodies. In cold weather we go to the public bathhouse, which is open every day. But now when I'm not there, Fengyun must ask somebody to take Ze to the men's bathhouse.

To escape the dullness of my room I began to walk, several times a day, to the shore of Lake Michigan. After that short walk of five minutes, I would continue along the bike track skirting the shore. Crabapples still hung on the trees in clusters. In Beijing these trees would long ago have been bare, the children not sparing them. The grass was still green in the park along the lake and on the lawns in front of the lovely houses bordering on Sheridan Road. I couldn't understand why American grass was green all year around. Perhaps it is because the soil is so rich that the grass is very strong, just as Americans can stand cold because they have so much food. How little they wear—even in winter, only one layer of clothing, a jacket under an overcoat. The women seem to wear sandals and skirts in all the seasons.

Most of the days I found hardly anyone on the beach, only a few joggers. (Americans will spend an hour jogging, but will usually drive to work over a distance they could cover in twenty minutes by walking.) Occasionally a car would pass and a dog might bark from its open window. I felt comforted, then abandoned as they moved into the distance. The lake was so large that I could have mistaken it for an open sea. The waves rolled into shore, helped along by the wind blowing from the east. In some places the large breakers dumped foam up over the rocks. Standing there in the wind, looking out over the huge expanse of water, gave me some moments of exultation.

One Sunday morning I saw a middle-aged man walking slowly along the beach, holding something that resembled a mine detector. Out of curiosity and the urge to speak a few English sentences, I went up to him. He explained that this was his hobby. He came to the beach every weekend to look for lost coins. "This is a metal detector," he said, indicating the instrument in his hand. "When it is held over a piece of metal, it buzzes." As he spoke, it buzzed. The man took a small spade out of his pocket and dug into the sand. He scooped up a rusty iron chip. As I walked with him for a distance of about twenty yards, he stopped four times to dig into the sand, finding nothing.

"How much does a metal detector cost?" I was trying to prod him into conversation.

"My wife bought it for me as a birthday gift. It costs somewhere around a hundred dollars."

A hundred dollars to buy a machine to look for pennies! How strange these Americans are. I wondered how long it would take to pick up enough money to pay for the detector. Fengyun would never buy a thing like that for me, nor would she send me out alone on the beach. This man must have had a maid to clean his house and wash his clothes. And his wife probably bought a toy for him to play with so he wouldn't bother her. I wished him "good luck"—a phrase I had recently acquired. I sincerely wished he might find a gold coin lost by some early settler.

The man concentrated on his search as I turned to walk back up to the McKnight's home, along the wide street. I wondered if people in these houses I passed knew how we lived in China. Later, after a year of going to many gatherings in American homes, I would become painfully conscious of the small size of our Chinese dwellings.

In the 1950s, before the housing situation in Beijing became so crowded, I had lived in my father's house in a large courtyard with flower beds and several flowering trees. Our family of six (my parents, two brothers, a sister and myself) used five of the rooms. But Beijing had become the capital and was developing rapidly. Government offices were expanding and factories were being built. The population of Beijing increased from two million in 1949 to five million by the end of the 1950s. Housing construction, however, could not keep pace. In 1956, my father's colleagues decided that we had too many rooms. In a rage, my father moved us out of the old residence and into a three-room house.

After I married Fengyun, we lived for almost twelve years in a sixteen-foot square single room, in an old-fashioned Beijing courtyard house. Eleven families lived in the dozen rooms around the courtyard, which held several little shacks, providing a place for the children to play hide-and-seek games. The Foreign Languages Press, which owned the property, built a makeshift, outdoor kitchen for every household. We all shared the two water taps in the yard, one of which had to be shut off in the winter, and the other moved near a coal stove to keep the pipes from freezing. The toilets, used in turn by eleven families—forty people—often froze in winter.

We were able to move out of our one-room house in 1980, into a newly built, high-rise building. How happy Fengyun was when she saw the huge bedroom—16 x 20 feet—and a small one for our young son. How proud Ze would be to tell his classmates that he had a room of his own. We finally had a kitchen and toilet inside our home, and Feng-yun kept everything clean and neat.

The new apartment was comfortable and private. I was no longer bothered by the shouts of children in the courtyard while I read. After a while, however, I began to be bothered by the quiet. When we had lived in the old courtyard, we could always have a chat with neighbors on summer evenings. While our son ran around the yard, we ate out-of-doors and often sampled food from another family's table. We could see what our neighbors were doing through the uncurtained windows, and we grew to know each other intimately. When Fengyun and I went out, we could leave our son with any of our neighbors and know that they would take care of him. In the new high-rise, we were confined by the concrete walls. Our son missed his pals from the old courtyard and had to play by himself in our rooms. In life, there's gain and there's loss. Nothing can be perfect.

Our apartment was the best among the homes of my eighteen colleagues. Only two or three of us had a place large enough to allow our foreign friends to visit. We moved into this apartment just in time to entertain Ron for dinner. Giving a dinner for a foreigner is a serious matter in China. I went to the largest grocery in Beijing and ordered ready-to-cook dishes at a special counter, stating that I would use them to entertain a foreign guest. The clerk was impressed and gave me the freshest meat and fish and the cleanest vegetables. The dinner for Ron cost two-thirds of my monthly salary, but we were happy because we had a place where we could express our friendship.

● ● ●

I had had a family of my own for many years and I was used to being my own master under my own roof. Though the McKnights treated me well, I didn't feel at ease. I was always conscious of being an outsider and an intruder into their family life. All the members of the family went out of their way to please me, but their politeness kept me from understanding them better. Whenever I came into

22

the living room in the evening and saw the McKnights talking, I didn't know whether I should stay or leave. I very much wanted to watch TV programs so that I could train my ear, but my mind couldn't concentrate with the family sitting around and I felt I should never stay too long with them. I had the feeling that my presence kept them from really relaxing.

Ingar, the family dog, barked at me and jumped on me when the McKnights were home. That was not the way she treated the family members. Yet she was very quiet when the McKnights were out, lying calmly in a corner. I did not like this dog—I knew she was not an honest dog, but I had to pretend to like her to show my respect for the family.

One Saturday Professor McKnight drove me around Evanston and the surrounding area. He showed me the campus of Northwestern University and pointed out the red brick building that is the Medill School of Journalism. It stands at the southern end of the campus, dwarfed by the openness of the parking lot and intersection before it. I was in awe of its fame, but it did not look as magnificent as I had expected. We passed the Bahai Temple and continued along Lake Avenue. All around us were imposing mansions. Professor McKnight pointed north, telling me that ahead was the village of Kennilworth, "Entirely WASP." He explained the abbreviation as standing for "white, Anglo-Saxon Protestant." "Lily white" was a term I learned later.

• • •

Now that I was in a foreign country, I realized that I might become somewhat defensive—if Americans were to say critical things about China. Back in Beijing, my colleagues and I had raised many criticisms of the Chinese government and expressed them openly. But when Mrs. McKnight would occasionally make jokes about the backwardness of China, I reacted with resentment. Once, when they were having a problem with mice in their kitchen, I set traps and caught seven of them in succession. In praise of my heroic deed she said, "You have a billion people in China. How many mice do you have?"

I flared up. "You should not make fun of my country. You hurt my feelings when you joke about China."

She apologized and told me she was trying to make me feel better. But how could I enjoy such jokes? I was very sensitive on such matters, and viewed any disparaging remark about China as a personal affront. I would later come to understand and accept "kidding" from Americans as something they generally reserved for people they liked.

In these days I looked for any distraction and sometimes offered my help, cleaning the stove or the dishwasher. The hot air inside the house, heated by a "closed-circuit" system, bothered me so much I welcomed a snowfall as an excuse to go outside to sweep the porch and shovel the sidewalks. Sometimes I stayed outside and took a short walk along their street—short because as I walked along, I had the feeling of being an outcast, completely alone in some deserted city. Occasionally cars drove past, but there were no other people walking on the concrete sidewalks. In Beijing, I had become skilled at maneuvering myself quickly through the crowd of people blanketing most streets. It never occurred to me that walking alone, with a whole sidewalk to myself, would require a greater skill.

During these days of waiting for school to begin, I had nowhere else to go but out to the lake. And there I often stood, looking at the white domes, spires and lofty rooftops of Northwestern University. One afternoon I walked north, thinking I might look inside the campus. But I stopped after I had entered the gate and gone fifty yards; a feeling overwhelmed me, a feeling that I had lost something that I couldn't name. Depression weighed me down, and all around me was a deadly quiet. I felt I was on the property of some wealthy man, without his permission. It was as if I were afraid of being accused of stealing. I walked out through the gate, holding myself back from running. I felt the occupants of the elegant houses along Sheridan Road gazing at me from behind curtains. The richness of the place overwhelmed me. I was a stranger in this place and did not belong here.

I stopped to look out again across the cold blue lake. Again it soothed me. The waves, the wind, the desolation were the cure for my depression.

CHAPTER THREE

WINTER CELEBRATION

Christmas in America is said to be a holiday for children, but as I experienced the celebration of this holiday for the first time, it appeared to be more of a time for adults. The McKnights were planning to give a party and had invited me to go with them to the parties of others. Through these occasions I would begin to see the life of the American middle class and the wealth of this consumer society. The extravagance exceeded even the scenes I had read about in novels, scenes of the celebrations of very wealthy families and imperial courts in ancient China.

Christmas preparations at the McKnights began a few weeks before the holiday, and this gave me something to do with my time, something to occupy my mind. For nearly a whole morning Mrs. McKnight and I carried dozens of boxes down to the living room from the attic on the third floor, boxes of colorful light bulbs and ornaments for the Christmas tree. One big carton contained a hundred eggnog cups, brought out for use only once a year at their Christmas party. I found this amazing. For several years I had wanted to buy just four stemmed glasses so we would not have to drink wine from tea cups.

Another afternoon we spent polishing silverware, bowls, plates and candelabra, like beautiful pieces I had seen in films. Americans have countless dinner table and kitchen articles. In my kitchen, and in at least 90 percent of the Beijing homes, there are two cleavers, a dozen pairs of chopsticks, a dozen plates and bowls, a half dozen soup spoons and several fine porcelain plates reserved for special occasions—that's all. I would love to have some of the tools in American kitchens: exquisite peelers, a set of stainless steel knives hanging on a magnetic rack, electric mixers, and especially that marvelous invention, the food processor. But I am a practical man and know that even if I could afford to buy those luxuries, I would not have space for them. My kitchen would barely hold a refrigerator, and I prefer to keep the space in my bedroom for my books.

The first party the McKnights took me to, in Chicago, was hardly a pleasant experience. The day was freezing cold and I felt carsick as we drove along the beautiful Lake Shore Drive on the way downtown. The wind was blowing in from the lake, brisk and chilly. Even Professor McKnight's enthusiasm, as he pointed out the view of the city, failed to cheer me. The skyline was rugged-looking with all the buildings and lights. On the dark horizon to the east, a red signal light flashed gloomily on top of the dim silhouette of Navy Pier. I shivered. I recognized the John Hancock Building looming sharply over the dark and tall buildings. Before I left Beijing, Ron Dorfman had proudly shown me a picture of this second tallest building in Chicago. He had an apartment on the eighty-sixth floor. What would it be like living so high, I wondered. He told me about the thirty miles of parks and beaches here along the lake, and I had looked forward to seeing such a beautiful place. Now nothing impressed me and I felt no elation.

We came onto Michigan Avenue—one of the richest

streets in the richest country in the world, a millionaire's street, the "golden mile." The avenue was packed with holiday shoppers; trees glistened with shimmering lights; store windows were shining and colorful. I would have a lot to talk about later, but now my mind was slow and dull. I was frozen.

We stopped somewhere near the Loop at the entrance to an old apartment building. Professor McKnight checked the name plates at the entryway and pushed a button. The door buzzed. We went inside and took an elevator to the thirteenth floor. Like most elevators in America this one did not have an operator. That would be unheard of in Beijing, where children would no doubt play in them and, before too long, they would break down. My five-story office building had one elevator and it was exclusively reserved for foreigners. Chinese, old and young, climbed the stairs. But in time, many of the foreign workers who felt uncomfortable at having special privileges, enthusiastically started climbing with us.

We emerged into a gorgeous apartment. The hostess took our coats and ushered us into a room where drinks and food were being served. On the table were a big punch bowl, a coffee urn, and dishes full of cookies, fruit and many foods I didn't recognize. I followed the example of the McKnights and filled a paper cup with punch, and picked up slices of raw vegetables and several cookies. I sampled other foods, but only some did I like.

From time to time a maid collected the paper cups and plates scattered all over the room on chairs and window seats. She dumped them into a trash bag, half-filled with wasted food and drink. I could not understand such wastefulness, even after I had been in the United States for a long time and had gone to many parties. In school cafeterias, in restaurants and even in offices, one could pick up as many paper napkins, plates, plastic forks and spoons as one liked, and no one paid the slightest attention.

Apparently these things are worth nothing in this country. In China, the government pays subsidies to people who collect old newspapers, wastepaper, broken bottles and bones for recycling. Perhaps, if Americans didn't throw these products away, the people who make new ones would have to stop working.

A black woman in a red maid's uniform came over with more food on a tray, but I was too shy to take any. After the maid had passed us, Mrs. McKnight, who knew I loved seafood, told me I had missed the shrimp on the tray. I turned and stretched out my hand, but the maid didn't notice me and moved on. One of the guests saw this and laughed. I must have looked somewhat silly, not catching the maid's attention. Yet, I was not here to be laughed at and anger swelled inside me. Yes, I had come from a poor country, had never dealt with maids and had never experienced so-called society. But that was no reason to make me a laughing stock. I had to restrain myself from leaving.

I sat quietly then, by myself, and wondered about this country, these people, this winter celebration, all so different from my homeland. I remembered so well the Spring Festival of my childhood in the countryside. The Spring Festival, or New Year by the Chinese lunar calendar, falls in February and is the biggest Chinese holiday. Children can hardly wait for this holiday to arrive, with its gifts and good food.

• • •

Preparations for the Spring Festival began on the twentieth of January. My mother and aunts would cook chunks of meat, basins of fish and hundreds of steamed buns, stuffed with sweetened bean paste. This food, stored in big jars in the courtyard, was enough to sustain our whole family of thirteen for at least a month. On the eve of the festival, the women made hundreds and hundreds of meat dumplings for us to eat throughout the night and all the next day.

29

Early the next morning before I wakened, my grandfather would go to the country fair to buy us gifts. When the winter sun rose to the top of the tall old willow tree, my mother allowed me to go outside and wait for him on the stone bridge by the south gate to our compound. I could hear the noise of the street beyond the gate and waited excitedly, anticipating the gifts he would bring me. The snow-covered fields, stretching far and wide to the south, contained dark ugly patches. Animal-drawn carts passed silently by on the white wilderness of the country road. And then, from around a turn in the road, I saw grandfather's brown mule drawing his cart toward me. I was proud that our cart had rubber tires instead of wooden wheels like those of the other carts in the village. And it was drawn by a sturdy mule, instead of a donkey or an ox. Grandfather was perched on the seat, complacent as ever, as he could be with two sons—my father and Second Uncle—sending cash every month from their jobs in town. He was better off than anybody else in the hundred families in the village. From behind me I heard the cheerful hooting of my Third Uncle, the only one of my grandfather's three sons left to tend the family farm.

"Let me ride!" I shouted, running along the frozen road toward the cart.

Third Uncle came running, fished me up and threw me into the arms of my grandfather, without slowing up the cart.

"Did you buy firecrackers for me? Did you buy paper lanterns? I want a diablo, too!" I searched among the packages and baskets on the cart for this toy with a devilish ball to balance on a string between two sticks.

"Of course, I bought everything you wanted," my grandfather laughed. I was his treasure, and I knew it. I was his eldest son's eldest son, his heir and direct line on the family tree.

Through the village street, lighted with large lanterns, I

30

ran and shouted with the other children, setting off fire-crackers and showing off our paper lanterns.

After I moved to the city and grew up to have my own family, Spring Festival became an occasion for visiting relatives. And although we always had good dinners, visiting my family one day, my wife's family another, the excitement and the grandeur were gone.

• • •

I went with the McKnights to many parties, not because I enjoyed them, but because I needed to know about American culture—pride or no pride. I felt I was being looked down upon, humbled, and yet, I had to go in order to learn. It would take a longer time for me to become more aggressive, to be proud, as proud as anyone present at any gathering.

At one of these pre-Christmas parties I met again Leon Despres. As this slender gentleman in his late sixties approached me with a glass of wine, I was embarrassed not to recall his name or where I had met him. He reminded me that we had met and talked for a few minutes once when he came to visit Ron Dorfman in my Beijing office. How could I have forgotten! I remembered that this energetic former Chicago alderman had detached himself from a tourist group, borrowed a bicycle, and ridden it through the side streets of Beijing. Professor McKnight told me that Mr. Despres was now serving as parliamentarian for the city council. "An important man," he said. "Right next to Mayor Byrne."

Mr. Despres invited me to sit in on the next session of the Chicago City Council, on December 21, and I accepted. When the twenty-first came, it was a bitter cold day. Layers of frost blurred the windows in my room. I hesitated about whether to put on my woolen underwear. Houses in the United States are too warm for that; you can take off a woolen sweater in somebody's house, but not underwear. In Beijing, everyone wears underwear throughout the winter because the buildings are not overheated. I decided against it—after all, when in Rome, do as the Romans do (or

31

at least try to understand why they do it, and adjust).

I was going to take the elevated train to Chicago. A strong wind blew against me while I stood waiting on the platform next to the tracks. I began to shiver and regretted not having put on the underwear. A middle-aged woman came up from the ticket office and pushed a button on the side of the glass shelter. The lights above me came on and I felt a stream of heat. Americans certainly know how to take care of themselves.

The train finally arrived and after a short ride, I had to get off and change to another train, at the Howard Street platform. So, before I had stopped shivering in the heated Evanston train, I found myself standing outside again in the freezing cold. On this longer ride of the North-South train, it took about five minutes for me to thaw out. As soon as I emerged from the subway at Washington Street, the cutting wind struck again.

I hurried west on Washington, passed Daley Center Plaza, and got lost. I asked directions from a policeman, a black man of about fifty. Cordial and patient with my broken English, he walked me to the entrance of the City Hall which loomed right in front of me. Inside, at the entrance to the Council Meeting hall, a guard came up and asked if I were Mr. Liu. He said, on Mr. Despres's instructions, that he was expecting me. I was impressed and felt flattered. The guard showed me to a seat in the large hall.

Mr. Despres came over and gave me a briefing on what was going to be debated that day: patronage policy and some bills. He handed me a thick volume of the last council meeting's records. I was excited when he told me he was going to introduce me to Mayor Byrne. I admired the sharp tongue and quick mind of this woman who was mayor of one of the largest cities in the United States. But I was to be disappointed; she left early for another meeting.

The council meeting was more disorderly than anything I could have imagined. The fifty aldermen and alderwomen entered and left the meeting room at will; some of the remaining ones chatted and laughed together in small groups. Occasionally, one would stand up to speak to those in their seats, and once in a while the secretary would call the roll for a vote. Often he had to raise his voice and repeat the name of some alderman who had gone out into the lobby for a cup of coffee or a cigarette. I had seen documentary films of Japanese congressmen engaging in fist fights, and I had read of Englishmen in Parliament shouting names at one another. But I had not expected such behavior from those who are elected to be representatives of the people.

There were several elements of the council meeting that seemed to have little relationship to the making of legislative decisions. The meeting was opened by a small orchestra, after which the master violinist came to the rostrum and played a special tune for the mayor. Then a basketball team was presented to the council and received a citation from the mayor because they had won a game. A beautiful black woman was introduced to the council because she had won the title, "Miss Black America." One of the aldermen made a speech, inviting her jokingly for dinner; everybody laughed. I could not understand why these people took their business so lightly. Later, a friend told me that all important legislative decisions are made outside the meeting hall.

I had difficulty following the speeches, and soon I lost interest. After Mayor Byrne left, I lapsed into my own thoughts. The session went on until noon. Mr. Despres apologized for not being able to take me to lunch, since he had another meeting. We walked together through a tunnel to the subway station, without being exposed to the cold outside. The whole morning taught me two things: there is a tunnel from City Hall to the Washington subway station, and, Despres didn't have a car and is a man close to the mayor.

Ron Dorfman returned from Beijing a few days before Christmas. We embraced, and tears came to my eyes. He had come from the place where my people were. He was dear to me; he was the only one in the United States whom I had known before I had entered this strangeness. Eagerly I accepted the invitation to go with him to Irene Turner's country house in Michigan for a long holiday weekend. And how grateful I was for this distraction from the increasingly depressing surroundings of Evanston.

We drove around the southern tip of Lake Michigan on the way to the house. With us were Irene Turner, a technician at Rush Memorial Hospital in Chicago; Don Rose, a writer and political consultant, and his family; and Al Jordon, a black middle-aged man working for the government. Along the way Irene pointed out to me the gigantic steel mills of Gary, Indiana, and she explained the tollway system that helps pay the cost of building U.S. highways. I still can't stop marveling over the skill and foresight of American highway designers and engineers. Thirty years after this highway network was completed, it is still adequately serving the ever-increasing load of traffic for the new, much-more-economically advanced society. If for no other reason, President Roosevelt should be remembered for starting this magnificent project.

Since we were going to stay in a country house, I was expecting to see some rural life. We arrived in the early afternoon to find three men fishing through tiny ice holes on the nearby solidly frozen lake. The scene was breathtaking: a ruggedly built house standing alone on the edge of a small lake surrounded by heavily wooded hills.

The brick house was lined inside with raw planking. A wooden stairway, supported by wooden pillars, led to the second floor. Everything was raw and unfinished, without elaborate decoration. Before long, however, I found out that all the comforts of the city were there: a gas heat system, electric stove, large refrigerator, electric coffee pot, food processor, electric can opener and, of course, sets of plates and glasses. The two bathrooms as well as the kitchen sink had hot water all the time.

Irene soon went off to buy a Christmas tree. The Roses had brought all the decorations for it. Entertained by music from a stereo, we hung the colorful balls, tassels and ornaments on the tree. Then everyone, but me, took beautifully wrapped boxes and packages from their traveling bags. Damned fool; I cursed to myself. How could I have not brought Christmas gifts? Though this was my first Christmas, I should have known it would be an occasion for gifts. That evening they drank and joked and played a game called Boggle as I watched silently.

The next day was Christmas. In the morning I told Irene I wanted to go to the lake to watch the people fishing. She said I should stay until we exchanged gifts. The thought of watching others give gifts horrified me. How embarrassing that would be! But it would be impolite to leave, so I stayed.

Don Rose was chosen to distribute the gifts that had been placed under the tree. He was thoughtful, I mused, to choose one gift for each person present. I received one, too. I couldn't identify my feelings—self-pity or resentment?

By the end of the gift giving, I had received several books from Al Jordon and the Roses, a pen stand from Irene, and a pair of blue jeans and leather belt from Ron. Before I left China, Ron had told me to get a pair of blue jeans. "You won't be American if you don't wear blue jeans," he said. I looked around in Beijing stores but couldn't find a pair. Ron bought me this pair as soon as he returned to the United States.

The day after Christmas there was a medium snowfall. Though the surroundings were now more charming in the snow, Ron's friends didn't go out. They drank, ate, played Boggle, and drank. I began wondering what they were here for. They could do this in their city dwellings. The next day I asked Ron to go with me for a walk.

The sky had cleared up. The winter sun was beating down lazily and the snow on the road along the hilly terrain was melting, partly from the heat of the sun and partly from the exhaust of the cars. The air was refreshing. Ron and I talked about what had happened in my office since I had left. As he talked about Lailai's marriage and Zhang Zhimei's difficulty finding a place for her family, I longed to see them again.

Along the road, which stretched up and down over the slopes, were dense virgin woods. Dead and fallen trees lay entangled on the ground to rot. Americans complain about the energy shortage while dead trees go to waste. I remembered my childhood when the villagers burned the stalks and roots of the crops for cooking and heating. Coal was expensive and not many peasants could afford it. Wood was rare, more expensive than coal. In autumn, children were sent out to rake up dry grass for fuel. Now the people in my native village earn more money, but coal is rationed by the government and is saved for industrial use. On the north China plains, wherever there are trees, there is certain to be a village. One rarely could come across woods in a natural state, the kind I saw so often when I later traveled through the United States.

During that long weekend, Ron and I prepared a Chinese dinner for the group. Having been in China, Ron thought of himself as an expert on Chinese cooking. Two months after he had arrived in Beijing he gave a party and I watched him prepare the dishes with a Chinese cookbook open on the window sill. I told him he couldn't cook with just a book. He said it was no problem. His beef dish was tough because he had stir-fried the meat with only a small amount of oil, as the book had directed, but I would have deep-fried the meat in half a pot of oil. He poured the used oil into the sink—that would be regarded as a sin by any Chinese.

Our joint-venture Chinese dinner at the country house was successful. Irene used her fingers to get the last bit of gravy from the plate. Later, I saw many Americans doing the same at other meals, but it is considered bad table manners in China. The mother always tells her child not to use his or her fingers while eating. "You will bring worms into your tummy," she would say.

There were many American customs which puzzled me. I was very impatient with table formality. Why do people have to remember to change plates, forks, knives, and spoons so many times in one meal? I was especially bothered by that piece of cloth called a napkin. English gentlemen tuck a white napkin under their chins during a meal and Americans put one on their laps. I had trouble remembering to do this even a year and a half after I had arrived and had been to a number of fancy restaurants. Even if I did place it on my lap, it always slipped onto the floor. I often remembered to use my napkin only when I saw someone wipe his mouth with one; I then hastily picked mine up and spread it across my lap, stealing a look to see if others had noticed my lack of etiquette.

On our last evening in the country, we drove for half an hour to Michigan City to have an Italian dinner. It was bitter cold and the road was covered with snow. The parking lot was full. We waited in a parlor for twenty minutes before we got our table. I told Ron to order anything for me but cheese. After a long rich meal with many courses, Don Rose took out a calculator to figure out how much each person owed for the meal. He collected the money across the table. I felt strange—we Chinese would never do it that way.

● ● ●

Christmas parties and celebrations had come to an end. People again settled down to the routine of their lives, but I had nothing to do but hang around the McKnight's house. I was counting the days, hoping that they would pass quickly and school would begin, so that I would have something to occupy my mind. Perhaps school would give me more of a feeling of fitting in here, and a sense of purpose.

CHAPTER FOUR

MAKING FRIENDS

January arrived and school began. While Ron was in Chicago for the Christmas holiday, he had made arrangements with Vernon Thompson, a professor and assistant dean at Medill School of Journalism, for him to be my academic advisor. Professor Thompson worked out a plan of study for me, and asked that I report to him once a week. During the winter quarter, according to this plan, I was to read independently, to audit various regular courses, and to familiarize myself with the new environment. But on the first day of classes, I knew this was not the place for me. I was at least a decade older than most of the students, spoke poor English and was the only Chinese in the classrooms. I was not making a good adjustment to the school.

Professor Thompson assigned me several thick books on the American news media. If I had been in China, I would have sat down immediately to read them all, eight hours a day, until I was finished. But I wanted to take more advantage of my surroundings, to meet and talk with people, to begin to understand American society and culture. I needed to improve my ability to speak and listen in English. The books he gave me to read, on theories of U.S. journalism, had little relationship to my job back in China—the political and economic systems are too different. So I read the books sporadically, attended classes, and sought other means of learning.

I met my first real American friend one afternoon when I went to Professor Thompson's office for a conference and found him talking to Victor Valle, a 34-year-old Mexican-American student. Professor Thompson introduced us and after talking for awhile, Victor invited me to his home for dinner on the weekend. There I met Mary, his wife, who had a Chinese grandfather, and who seemed glad to welcome me every time I visited. In my talks with Victor, he advised me that I should learn to be "aggressive" in this country, or I would get nowhere. How to be aggressive? It took me all of a year to understand how to be that way.

Through Victor I received my first invitation to a Professor's home. Victor told me one day when we met on campus that Jay Harris, a talented black professor at Medill, wanted me to come to his home for dinner. I was flattered to have a personal invitation. The next day an attractive black woman in her early thirties stopped me in the corridor and introduced herself as Christine, Professor Harris's wife. She was also a professor at Medill. She described to me where they lived and how I could get there. She even offered to pick me up in her car, but I told her I would come by bicycle.

The dinner was to start at seven o'clock. I set out on my bike at six and rode south along the lake front. Dusk was falling when I came to a dead end. I looked at the numbers on the building doorways, but I was lost in the darkness. I asked directions from two people walking along the lake, and they said that 497 Sheridan Road, the Harrises' address, was twenty blocks south. This didn't make much sense to me—how long was a block?

I turned around and retreated back to the school and called the Harrises' house. I had intended to save them trouble, but only succeeded in causing confusion since they had to make a special trip to get me. Damn my pride! It took fifteen minutes by car to their house, which was miles south of where I had stopped.

It was a minority get-together: Victor, a Mexican, and his wife, Mary, a Mexican with a Chinese grandfather; a Chinese-American named David; the black Professor Harris and his wife, Christine, herself a black with German blood; and I, pure Chinese. The subject that inevitably arose before the evening ended was the treatment of minority students. Victor had a lot to complain about, but I had been in the United States for too short a time to take a position.

That evening we also discussed the matter of ethnic identity. I asked Professor Harris how he thought of himself, as an American first, or as a black first? After a moment's thought he said, "Black first." I could not understand why American blacks searched for their African roots. After all, they had been born and had lived in the United States for many generations. They were not newer than any of the other peoples, and they had a large population. To an outsider it seemed that blacks would be better off if they were to put more stress on educating their own people and less on blaming others for their lack of opportunities.

I later asked a black woman who was a guest speaker at Northwestern, "American blacks are Americans. They have lived in this country as long as whites, American culture is their culture—why do they think they are different from whites?" My question was well-intentioned, my thinking that people who have shared a culture for so long should have a comon feeling for it. She said I was right to some extent; blacks should take American culture as their own, but in American culture there is a lot of prejudice against blacks. "Do you know who has the power?" she asked. I didn't.

At a Christmas party I had asked a white woman, "How do you feel about the fact that the black population is growing fast while the white population is declining? Do you think Americans might one day elect a black for president?"

"No," she answered. "We know how to keep the power."

She didn't tell me how. After a year's stay in the United States I knew the country better and realized she was telling the truth. Although Chicago's population is 40 percent black, I didn't see many black students in the universities. Most of them lived in the poverty-stricken inner-city ghetto. Many of them have lived on social welfare for so long that they have lost a sense of value for education and work. Sometimes I suspected that the ruling class was deliberately keeping black people in an inferior position to whites.

• • •

A pleasant young woman who sat next to me in my News Writing class invited me to go with her to a blues concert early the next Friday evening. I didn't know what blues was, but I eagerly accepted because I was desperately in need of company. Since the start of the session we had been talking for a few minutes before and after class, and she was sympathetic with my plight of trying to live in a foreign country since she had lived in Germany for a year. She wrote out her name for me—Sue Lestingi.

We arrived early at the concert hall and, as usual, I felt out of place. We chatted fitfully, jumping from one subject to another. We discussed the weather in Beijing, compared to Chicago. She asked me about my family and, since I had the largest vocabulary in this topic, I told her everything I could think of, in great detail. I didn't know whether or not to ask her about her family. From what she offered to tell me, I learned that she was twenty-seven, unmarried, sharing an apartment near the campus with another student, and working in a restaurant to support herself.

The concert began with a half-hour lecture on blues music by a music professor from the University of Illinois at Chicago Circle. Because my English comprehension was still weak, I didn't gain much knowledge about this kind of music from the lecture. Then five performers came on stage—a pianist, a drummer (the only white man), two guitarists, and the singer. The dull melody of the guitars and piano was stifled by the loud, monotonous rhythm from the drums. I had developed a great dislike for rock and roll music when Jonathan and his friends practiced their drums and guitar in the basement every afternoon. This noise also grated on my nerves.

Sue turned toward me and asked how I liked it. I was afraid I might disappoint her. I told her it was OK. I was learning. At half-past-five there was a break, and Sue said she really should get back to work at the restaurant. I suspected that she was not so interested in the music either. I walked part of the way with her to her job, then said goodbye.

I had been noticing that many of the students had jobs and I admired the way they were going through school, earning the money themselves. On campus I saw them working everywhere—in the library, the cafeteria, the secretarial offices. Later I found out that few American college students depend financially on their parents. Most of them get loans from the government, or they work to pay their way. I was told that many well-to-do families let their young children earn pocket money by baby-sitting or selling newspapers. This was good; in these ways they would learn the value of labor from an early age.

Even if students in China wanted to work, they would find no jobs, either on the campus or outside. All the work in the universities is done by permanently-hired staff members. Chinese universities don't charge tuition and most of the students receive some kind of financial subsidy from the school. Parents pay the balance of the board and other costs.

● ● ●

I had to find more friends. After several weeks in school I knew only a couple other students, and saw them only to talk to for a few minutes, perhaps three times a week. I decided I would get to know a few more names, at least, from my three classes. One day I came ten minutes early to my 11:00 A.M. News Media and U.S. Government class. Two young women, one black and one white, were already there. I told myself to be aggressive, as Victor advised me to be, and went up to them.

"Hi." I tried to be casual. "My name is Liu Zongren. I come from Beijing, China." I put stress on Beijing, hoping that might create some attention.

"Oh, really?" The white woman seemed interested. "How long have you been here?"

"Two months."

"How do you find it here?"

I couldn't understand what she meant. "I came here by plane, of course." I must have looked lost. The white woman added quickly, "I mean, do you like this country?"

"Well, I don't know." How foolish I was. Why had I said this?

"My name is Ann. This is Geri."

Geri was the black woman. She smiled at me. "I've learned Chinese."

"How nice," I smiled back. "How much do you know?" I was hoping this would make the conversation last longer than just a courteous exchange.

"I studied it only a few months and found it too difficult, so I dropped it."

"Yes, Chinese is a difficult language," I faltered, not knowing how to continue. You can carry on a little more, I told myself. "Do you like this class?"

The women nodded, "Yes." I cursed myself: why do you ask such a silly question? If they don't like it, why are they taking it? How stupid I am.

Several other students had come in by now and I didn't

know if the two women wanted to go on talking. I began feeling nervous when I realized that I was standing in the middle of the classroom.

Ann started to move away. "Glad to meet you, Mr. —"

"Liu," I said hastily. "Just call me Liu. My last, no, my first name is too hard to pronounce."

"Glad to meet you, Mr. Liu," Ann repeated.

"Thank you," I said to them, my face flushed. I wondered what I had thanked them for, as I made my way to a nearby seat.

After the class began, most of what the professor said escaped my ears and I left as soon as the lecture was over. I had no other class that day and I didn't want to go back to the loneliness of the McKnight house, so I wandered around the campus. Many students were entering a particular lecture hall. I stopped and checked my timetable. It was a history class. Good.

I went in. It was a large classroom with at least eighty students already there, and more coming in. I selected a seat not too close to the lectern. Nobody paid any attention to me and I saw several oriental faces among the crowd. I relaxed, took out my notebook, and opened the campus newspaper, pretending to be an old hand. A young man sat down beside me and smiled. My watch said it was five minutes until class. Perhaps I could strike up a conversation with this young, friendly-looking man. I started my routine. "My name is Liu Zongren. I come from Beijing, China."

"Glad to meet you. My name is George Christi." He seemed in the mood to talk.

"Please write down your name for me." I handed my notebook over to him. "You know, it is very hard for me to remember American names without seeing them spelled out." I said this out of a desire to speak two more sentences, rather than as an explanation. I looked at what he wrote. "Is yours the same name as that British woman detective writer?"

"Sort of," he answered.

"I like her books, although I don't read novels often."

Seeing me at a loss, he asked, "How do you like the weather here?"

"Much the same as that in Beijing. We have cold winters, too."

"I hope someday I can go to Beijing."

"You will surely be welcome. If you wait for two years, I can show you around." I was so very eager to make a friend of him.

Unfortunately, the professor appeared and the class began. I would be sure to come to this class again and locate this friendly young man.

I didn't try my luck anymore that afternoon. Instead I found a seat in the library and tried to finish some reading assignments for Professor Thompson. I took out my books, but my mind refused to register anything. I glanced around the nearly full library; some students were doing their homework, a few were dozing on the sofa along the wall. Looking at those tired students, I remembered an item in the campus newspaper reporting that the 1981 tuition would be $6,900. How could I blame the students for not wanting to talk to me? The costs were so high, they had to put their time and energy into their studies.

I put aside my books and began a letter to Fengyun, but I couldn't finish it. Disheartened, I packed up my books and walked slowly back to my room. I knew my misery came not only from missing my family, but also from the frustration of being unable to learn. People in Beijing must be thinking I was enjoying myself here in the richest country in the world. Yet I was suffering, not because people in America were rejecting me, but because they didn't understand me and didn't seem to care how I felt—and because I didn't understand them, either. After my three classes each day, I wandered around the campus like a ghost. I had nowhere to go.

I felt better when dusk fell, knowing that another day

had passed. I wished the nights could be longer and the days shorter. Only when I was asleep could I forget the anxiety, the terrible feelings of isolation and loneliness. At 5:30 the next morning I was awake, staring through the grey early light at the ceiling of my room, six-thousand miles away from home. I had slept only four hours. My brain was alert but I didn't want to think about anything. I yearned for the comfort of oblivion, but I was unable to fall asleep again, no matter how hard I tried. I turned on the bed light and propped myself against the pillow. I opened my book to the same twenty pages of *American Mass Media* that I had been reading for several weeks now. Reading might make me drowsy. I tried to concentrate.

I heard a familiar sound coming from under the door—I thought it must be the mouse that had come into my room before. Afraid of scaring my friend away, I slowed my breathing. From his scrambling sounds I could follow his path, climbing up my traveling bag, hanging there, and then jumping onto my bed. He crept over to my head, sniffed at my hair, and nudged my ear—his whiskers tickling my cheek. Then he climbed across my back and jumped onto the bedside table to nibble at my crackers. I moved slightly and he jumped down and raced under the door. I was sorry to disturb him; this ugly little creature was a welcome addition to life in that lonely room.

The room was getting lighter; Fengyun must be at work now, I thought. No, I'd better think about something else. What were yesterday's lessons? What had I learned? Professor Swashloe talked about freedom of the press. He said journalists should write objectively without committing themselves. But, in order to sell newspapers in the United States, they have to satisfy the taste of consumers. That is not exactly freedom of journalism. Is it, perhaps, the fate of journalists everywhere to have to take orders to some extent? American journalists have to follow the whims of their editors; Chinese journalists are smothered in the changing official policies. Reports on crimes? Scandals? What else? I couldn't remember. Damn it, we didn't report crimes that way in China. What did all this have to do with my job at *China Reconstructs?*

I looked at my watch—6:00 P.M. in Beijing. What was my son doing now? He and Fengyun must be on their way home. The curtains on my two windows began to reflect a pale whiteness that told me it was snowing again. I shivered, thinking of the twenty-minute walk to the campus at nine. I pushed this thought back into the depths of my mind. I remembered that in Fengyun's last letter, she told me they were having a few snowfalls. I hoped there would be very little snow in Beijing this year, as in recent years. Snow makes it difficult for Fengyun and Ze to go to work and school. She is still riding a bicycle through the busy streets, the half-hour it takes her from our home to her office. She might fall on the snow-covered road. Who would take care of her if she hurt herself? And Ze couldn't go to school by himself, since she takes him along to the school by our office building.

Someone walked past my door. It was Professor Mc-Knight going down to let Ingar out. I heard the door click and Ingar bark. It was time to get up and start another day of separateness, of what felt almost like exile.

I was beginning to consider my plight in terms of an African tribe I'd heard of, in which they had a peculiar punishment for high crimes. If a young man killed his wife, elders gave him the severest sentence: he was forbidden to talk to people. He was sent into the forest where he could find plenty of water and food for his survival. After two months, such a convicted criminal would usually return and plead to endure any hardship, as long as he might be allowed to remain among his people.

• • •

One mid-February night, when I absolutely could not stand my empty room any longer, I went out into the cold and walked the five minutes to the lake. The white breakers rushed against the shore and the rocks glistened with ice. Over the black eastern horizon of Lake Michigan was Beijing. My plane had flown over the lake. When could I fly back over it again? I ran along the snow-covered bicycle track, not feeling the biting cold or the harsh wind blowing at me off the lake. I shouted out the name of my wife, then cried, the tears streaming down my face. And this did not shame me.

I could have decided to go back home then. I could have written a letter to my office and told them that my health was not up to the intense study, and they wouldn't have objected. But I had to choose not to go back. All the money would be wasted if I went back without learning something. China is poor and foreign currency is badly needed for economic development. The government had spent $3,000 on my clothing and plane tickets and would have to pay another $1,500 for my ticket back. They had spent this money expecting me to learn things I could use to do a better job when I returned. And I did want to achieve something in my life. I should not give up so easily. No matter how hard my situation in the United States might be, I decided, I had to stay.

Two hours later, back in my room, I felt better. A little of the depression, accumulated over the past weeks, had been released. I slept well that night, dreaming of Fengyun, my son and myself watching TV together in our sparsely furnished apartment.

CHAPTER FIVE

A HORSE DOESN'T GRAZE
BACKWARDS

February was full of momentous events: The assasination of John Lennon was still in the news; Ronald Reagan became president; and the Amerian hostages were released in Iran. I sat in front of the TV for hours every day. How remarkable the scenes in Washington were, as the triumphant Reagan took his vows and the pitiful Jimmy Carter left the White House almost unnoticed. The highlight of Reagan's inauguration was the release from Teheran of the hostages. Reagan, the actor, as well as the man and politician, appreciated fully the drama of the homecoming. Carter must have cursed his own rotten luck. Why hadn't the Iranians released the hostages one day earlier? What a face-saver that might have been. I sympathized with Carter.

Newspeople had reason to rejoice. The editors didn't have to rack their brains to come up with subjects for news. The major stories just kept breaking one after another. For nearly two weeks, reporters were busy exploring every corner of John Lennon's life. By simply skimming the headlines, I learned that this great Beatle had a Japanese wife and a son, and found that the most intimate details of their lives were common knowledge.

That was a great lesson. Coming out of an oriental culture, I had never before even heard of the Beatles. In the United States, they were national heroes, more celebrated than President Carter. I had read and learned from *The Empire of Henry Luce* that the powerful news media can create presidents as easily as God made a woman from Adam's rib. Now I was watching the media transform one of the Beatles into a god. Some friends of mine told me that the Beatles had helped shape the American nation in the 1960s (Carter said something similar). When I expressed my bewilderment at the hysterical mourning for Lennon, my friends told me, "You didn't live in the United States in the 1960s." Well, perhaps that was the reason, but if I had, I don't think I would have developed such hero worship for a guitar player.

No sooner was Lennon laid to rest than the news machine started rolling again, this time covering the hostages and their families. As a foreign observer, I was moved by the show of patriotism on the part of Americans. I had come to believe that political concern was dead in this country, that people had so many material things to enjoy they had stopped caring about what was going on outside their comfortable homes.

But Americans were being very politically enthusiastic: rallies were held to welcome the hostages home; yellow ribbons were hung on cars and trees and buildings. However, the news media almost spoiled the event by reporting on and on, dragging too many details and too many people onto the scene. They not only bothered the hostages and their relatives, who refused to be interviewed, but also antagonized the veterans of Vietnam. The Vietnam vets resented the attention and warmth given the hostages. "We both suffered for our country," one group stated. "Why weren't we treated with the same respect?"

The sentiment against Iran was vehement. Many Iranian

students in the United States were sent home, the excuse being that their visas had expired. According to an article in the *Chicago Tribune*, the U.S. Immigration office was two years behind in its filing, which meant a student might stay unnoticed in the United States for two years beyond the expiration of his visa. Now the visas of Iranian students were being reviewed rapidly. And so, in addition to patriotism, I saw a tinge of xenophobia and heard occasional cries for isolation.

The new president's foreign policy became more and more aggressive. He threatened the relationship between the United States and China over the issue of arms sales to Taiwan. Some months later, in May, I and all the other visiting scholars from China received a notice from the Foreign Students Office demanding that we report to the State Department if we attended meetings and conferences in other cities. Did they think that we were spying? The State Department even asked university authorities to keep an eye on us, but the universities politely refused.

The new administration seemed to be saying to the rest of the world, "I am on the way. Follow me." The politicians urged that America protect its interests no matter where they were. And even though I liked the frankness of their speeches, it seemed as though many Americans acted as if they were still in the glorious days of the 1940s and 1950s, still believing that they could do anything they wanted in the world.

The Chinese have a proverb: "A rich man talks louder." America had long and arrogantly tried to keep power over others with its economic strength. Won't obey? Well, we won't give you grain, machines, or technology. They were trying to play God. Carter had used this kind of pressure and Reagan was now using it. The motto of Sun Yat-sen, the pioneer of the modern Chinese revolution, was, "Fight to stand equal among the nations of the world." I hoped that American politicians would someday learn from the words of this great third world leader.

• • •

Meanwhile more and more areas of my life were becoming meaningless. Two months had passed and I did not seem to be able to adjust very well to living in the McKnight's house. I wasn't sure whether I could survive for two years under these conditions. I began to wonder if it might be better for me to live with other Chinese. Before leaving China, I had decided not to speak Chinese at all in the United States, in order to make faster progress with English. And in these two months I had spoken more English than I had in all the fourteen years since I had been studying the language. Nevertheless, I now began to yearn to speak my own language again.

Professor McKnight kindly gave me the telephone number of a Chinese student at Northwestern, who gave me another number of a group of five Chinese living in an apartment west of the campus. They asked me to visit them on Saturday night. I knew none of them, but they looked, acted, thought, and spoke Chinese, and I felt comfortable and warm just being among my own people. After that, I went to their place every weekend, sometimes staying overnight. Perhaps I was speaking Chinese too much of the time, but with the tension gone I could relax, watch TV, and catch a lot more of the dialogue than at the McKnights. With these new friends I felt more safe and secure.

I tried going to more classes, as a way to pass the time. In the beginning, I would wait for the professor of the class to arrive to inform him that I was there to sit in. Later, I just went in and found a seat. Nobody seemed to care who was or wasn't there. Still the days were too long. For hours I would sit in a corner of the library, making every effort to focus on the books assigned to me by Professor Thompson. The words blurred as my thoughts drifted to the airplanes that passed overhead every half hour or so. Through the window I could see the snow melting under the early spring sun. Energetic, merry young people in pairs, and in threes and fours, hurried along in animated conversation. If only I could be one of them! I envied the students with oriental features who had American friends. By now I concluded that it was impossible for me to make friends with American students. There were too many differences between us. The age difference alone gave us different interests.

I tried to approach some professors. Professor Swashlose, who taught News Media and U.S. Government, had told the class that he was a believer in communism in the 1960s, and my impression from his lectures was that he was still interested in socialist countries. Since I came from a socialist country, I thought we might have something to talk about. I made an appointment to talk with him. However, the two talks in his office, each lasting about twenty minutes, made it clear that I wasn't making friends with this professor, either. No matter how friendly he tried to be, he gave me the impression that he was the professor and I was the humble student. The same age as I, he sat behind a big desk filling his pipe constantly, just as he did behind the lectern. I stumbled with my words, more because of my reaction to his status than because of my poor command of English.

Professor Swashlose, however, was a sensitive man in comparison to Professor Davis. This preeminent teacher at Medill had forty students in his News Writing class. Professor Thompson had particularly asked me to sit in on this class to learn the basic skills of news writing. Every morning at ten o'clock I slipped in to sit in a back seat, never daring to speak.

One day Professor Davis was lecturing on how to use question marks, saying that, according to the A.P. style, putting punctuation outside the quotes was the rule. According to *China Reconstructs* the rule is to put them inside. I knew in such matters there are different rules and that most writers don't really care. That day, however, I was tempted to speak out in class. I wanted to test my courage. I raised my hand, immediately conscious of the stares of the other students. I began to hope he would not see me.

"Well, go ahead," this sixtyish professor snapped.

Ignoring my pounding heart, I told him my magazine places punctuation inside the quotes.

"Your magazine? What's your magazine?"

I told him.

"Never heard of it!" he said. "I don't care whose rule it uses. You take my class, you listen to my rules."

Perhaps he was trying to be humorous, but I didn't think it was funny. All I recognized was his sarcasm. My face flushed, and my heart raced at a wild speed. "I am a foreigner," I wanted to say. "How dare you treat me so shabbily. If I have said something wrong, you, as the teacher, should correct me politely. This is the first time in one and a half months I have spoken in your class, and you embarrass me like this?" Oh, how I wished I could say those words aloud. I was furious and I felt frustrated, but I remained silent. "Under others' eaves you have to bend your head," a Chinese proverb says.

I began to wonder if I were attending the right school. Perhaps I should go elsewhere. There were several other universities in the Chicago area that were said to be good schools.

It was not an easy decision. I felt I was letting Ron and the McKnights down, after Ron had taken the trouble to get me into a good journalism school, and the McKnights had tried to please me. I wrote a letter to Ron, asking his opinion.

He replied: "I'm sorry you're having such a rough time. If you think it is your living situation that's creating the problem, then by all means, move. I assure you that neither Dean Cole nor the McKnights will be offended. Cole has nothing whatsoever to do with where you live, and the McKnights will certainly respect your judgement that you need a Chinese space in which to reassemble your thoughts after each day in an alien world. You're a grown man, and in America those kinds of decisions are entirely your own to make." He also said, "I think it is fairly common, when living in a foreign culture for the first time, to ride an emotional roller-coaster, with great highs and deep lows. That certainly has been my experience in China. For a long time you were my only real connection to China, and it was only on those occasions when I thought you had let me a little further into your life that my general state of gloominess was temporarily dispelled."

After a lot of mental struggle, I decided to transfer to the University of Illinois at Chicago Circle for two reasons. One was that the Chinese scholar Zheng Zhenyi, whom I had met in Beijing and with whom I had come to the United States, was studying computer science at Circle. He was getting along very well with American life, and he was a person I liked to be with. The other reason was that Zheng Zhenyi had taken me to see Judy Curry, a professor at the Speech and Hearing Clinic at Circle. He had told me how warm she was and how she had helped him with conversational English. I believed that she might help me as well.

In thinking about what to do with my future here, I had come to the conclusion that what I needed was a bridge person, one who could close the gap for me between the culture of China and the United States. There were a thousand things I was eager to know. The rest of my time in the United States would hardly be long enough to learn about the culture. I didn't want to be confined just to a classroom. I could take a hundred books back to read in my own country, but I couldn't take people with me. I had to know them here.

It hadn't taken long for me to realize that my language was not as much of an obstacle to learning as was my cultural heritage. Even if I could have understood all the words people were using in their conversations, I often had no idea what they were talking about. I could follow a conversation but could not take part in it because I knew so little about the subject. The gap was often so great that I thought we must be using different forms of logic in our thinking. As the Chinese say, "You can't grasp his mind."

Really, I should not have felt such great culture shock. For years I had been reading American novels, *Newsweek*, *Time* and *The Reader's Digest*. I was much more aware of American life than most other visiting Chinese scholars. I had had American teachers in school and had been exposed to American colleagues in my office. Perhaps the Japanese are right when they tell a foreigner who is unable to comprehend some of their ideas, "If only you were born Japanese, you would understand." I was born Chinese and so I think in a Chinese way.

My other difficulty was that the language used in daily life was quite different from that used in books. A foreigner can usually find the definition of a written word or phrase in the dictionary. However, many phrases used in daily conversation can be learned only through exposure to an environment in which people speak them constantly. Until one has learned how, it is even difficult to know how to order a dinner in an American restaurant. I heard of one Chinese professor who, having taught English for twenty years in a Chinese foreign language institute, didn't know how to order in a restaurant when he went to England with a delegation. As a translator, I needed this live language and experience. Chicago is a place saturated with lively English; Evanston was too quiet and too upper-middle class.

After having decided to move, I started looking for a sponsor at Circle. A friend introduced me to Dr. William Liu, Director of the Asian Pacific Mental Health Research Center, which is affiliated with Circle's sociology department. He helped me to transfer from Medill, and from the very beginning, I had a good impression of him. Dr. Liu had been able to preserve the Chinese virtue of modesty, in the midst of self-praising America.

Ten years my senior and much higher in social status, Dr. Liu accompanied me to get my identification card and to go through the procedures with the Foreign Students Office. Of medium height and proportionally built, he looked every part the scholar. He had come to the United States in 1946 at the age of sixteen as a student. Though he came from a wealthy family, he had worked his way through college, and before he went to Circle, he was the dean of a law and liberal arts school at another university.

I really wasn't expecting much from this move. But if I wanted to learn spoken English, it didn't matter whether I was going to prestigious Medill or to another school. Actually, I thought the best thing would have been for me to get a job where I could be involved constantly with Americans. Then I would learn to speak English most rapidly. Unfortunately, my passport didn't allow me to take a job. I remember a young New Yorker who came to China in 1966 to avoid the draft. After studying Chinese at a university for a year, he obtained work in a factory. At the beginning of 1969 he came to my office looking for a job. By then he spoke fluent Chinese and was an expert in the new romanized Chinese writing system.

To a certain extent I was pleased that I was finally learning to be more aggressive, to make my own choices, and to overcome the Chinese reluctance to say no to other people. I was doing what Victor had told me to do time and again. But before I had told the McKnights that I had decided to leave, I hesitated for several days. I worried that I would be letting them down if I left their house. And in the end, I didn't give them a straightforward reason; I only stressed the dullness of the school.

On a Saturday morning, Zheng Zhenyi came to Evanston to help me move. I can't put into words how I felt then. Bitter, miserable, regretful?—I didn't know. The McKnights probably were relieved that I was leaving. I must have become a bore to them—a depressed character hanging around their otherwise complacent life. They saw me off, without the many polite words that Chinese usually use when saying goodby to a guest. The white house stood quietly against the gray sky; the grass beside the sidewalks was turning tenderly green. It reminded me of the days I had swept the snow off their porch and sidewalk.

The train rumbled southward. It was Saturday and it was cold. The few passengers were wrapped in heavy coats, even though the car was heated. I began to realize that something was missing. I was here to learn about America and now I was moving away from an American family to live with Zheng Zhenyi and other Chinese. Where would I find the chance to speak English?

When the McKnights had said that I should feel free to come back to their house whenever I wanted to, I told them, a bit too bluntly, that if I didn't feel better in the new place I would go back to China. There wouldn't be any coming back. As the Chinese saying goes, a good horse doesn't graze backwards.

CHAPTER SIX

BEING AGGRESSIVE

The house at 814 South Claremont Street, where I had now moved, was a wooden frame building standing humbly next to a brick apartment building. Yang Lidan, Zhao Jian, Zheng Zhenyi and I had one bedroom, a huge living room and a kitchen on the first floor, and two bedrooms in the front part of the second floor. Margaret Shu, a Chinese-American nurse, who originally came from Taiwan, had the rear part of the second floor.

The ancient oil furnace in the basement consumed an outrageous amount of oil and gave off very little heat. The group had already paid out so much for their oil that, by the time I moved in, they didn't want to buy anymore. It was frequently colder inside than out. We wrapped blankets around our legs to keep warm and, after supper every night, walked fifteen minutes to the overheated Medical Center Library where we stayed until eleven o'clock, reading and napping. We did this until the days became warmer.

Our section of South Claremont Street was part of a small area in which the homes were owned by Italian immigrants, who rented them to university students. The area was surrounded by blacks and Mexican immigrants. The rent for our place was low—$60 per person, not including utilities. During the following winter, we each had to pay $120 a month, $40 of which went for heating alone.

The neighborhood was not very good-looking compared to Evanston's well-kept mansions and neatly cut lawns. Many of its vacant lots were overgrown with weeds, dry and shivering in the early spring winds. The cars parked on the streets were old models, with headlights missing and doors battered in. People on the streets were different from in Evanston—more blacks, Latinos and orientals than whites. In Evanston, I saw relatively few blacks.

The street along which we walked in the morning to reach the campus shuttle bus and back at night was littered with broken beer and wine bottles, cans, and garbage of all descriptions. Every time I turned the corner of Claremont onto Polk Street, two dogs barked ferociously, leaping at me behind a wire fence. The Circle campus itself was as gray as the houses around it—gray buildings, gray pavement, and students wearing dark glasses. However, I didn't stand out among those grays as I had in Evanston; the setting gave me camouflage.

When people asked me why I had left such a well-known school as Medill and a place as beautiful as Evanston, I told them that Evanston belonged to wealthy people, that I was not wealthy, and that I needed the kind of activities that Evanston lacked. A woman I knew in Evanston called to warn me that Chicago's west side was not the place for me. "It's too dangerous," she said. But a criminology professor at Circle said to me, "If you know where you are, you are safe in Chicago."

Shortly after I moved, I learned my first lesson about what it means to live in the city with the third highest crime rate in the United States. At four o'clock one afternoon, Zhao took a bag of garbage out the back door. No sooner had he dropped the bag in the trash bin than a black youth of about fifteen years of age came up and grabbed him, demanding money. Zhao was scared. He had heard others talking about people being stopped on the street for money, but he had never had a problem himself and never thought anything would happen in daytime. Zhao took out his wallet, thinking two or three dollars might pacify the young man. But the youth snatched the whole wallet and ran off.

Zhao, pausing a moment in astonishment, ran after him, shouting, "You have the money. Give me back my I.D. cards." Perhaps his English was not clear enough, for the black youth turned and threatened, "One step more and I'll kill you." Zhao stopped short. He understood the young man clearly, even though he could not make out every word. The youth vanished around a corner.

After that incident, two friends visiting us had bags and sweaters snatched at the same spot. We obviously had not learned how to cope with street crime. People advised us not to go to court to identify the criminals because they could get off easily and would then come after any witnesses. So we did not report the incidents to the police. Zhao applied for new I.D. cards.

There was one crime that we finally had to report. The victim was a Chinese woman who had been in Chicago only two months and was staying in our home temporarily. One afternoon, two of my roommates went with her to the post office, several blocks away. On their way back, two young black men approached them from behind and grabbed the purse the woman was carrying. In her purse were seventy dollars and her passport. She screamed. My two roommates turned around and ran after the youths, shouting, "Stop, thief!" The two purse snatchers disappeared into a housing project.

The day was clear and warm and people were coming and going, but nobody bothered to help. Children playing nearby just watched. My roommates felt indignant and silly at the same time. It was as if they were staging a comedy for an American audience. They now hesitated about whether or not they should go into the project after the thieves. They approached an elderly black man at the entrance to a building and told him what had happened.

"I saw all this," the old man said with sympathy. "You can't find them yourselves. Go and call the police." From his tone of voice, my roommates sensed that he knew who these young blacks were and that the police probably did also. They followed his advice.

Two policemen arrived in a squad car, and after taking a lot of notes, asked my roommates if they could identify the two black youths in court. My friends gave them a definite "no." One policeman smiled knowingly at the other and said to my friends curtly, "We'll do our best. If we find out anything, we'll be in touch with you." They never contacted us. The Chinese woman got a new passport a year later.

In China, the government would never permit the mugger of a foreigner to get away so easily. The public security department, from the top down, would make every effort until the culprit was caught and punished. Perhaps the problem in Chicago is that there are so many crimes the police have become indifferent.

When we first came from China we all had friendly feelings for blacks because the Chinese news media regularly reported on how our black brothers in the United States were oppressed. But, after a couple of months of living next to a black neighborhood, we began to develop a fear of them. When we were out walking, we tried to avoid the housing project inhabited by blacks.

I ventured into the project area only once when another roommate wanted to go to the post office there to mail a package. It was a Sunday afternoon and I went with him by bicycle from our street which was not far from the project. Yet as soon as we approached it I sensed, as well as saw, the difference in this neighborhood. There were many people about—adults and children—but the atmosphere was not as cheerful as the day was bright. A few boys were playing basketball in the parking lot in front of the post office.

I peeped into the entranceway of one building: its corridor was dark. We chained our bikes to a lamp post and went inside. The post office was a solidly built structure with heavy doors. A two-inch-thick sheet of plate glass blocked customers from reaching in over the counter. I urged my roommate to hurry.

The postal clerk opened a small door on a plate-glass box that was bolted to the window dividing the customers from the clerks. My roommate put his package into this box and the clerk locked its outer door and then opened the inner door on her side to take out the package. We paid the postage through a slot under the plate glass. Behind the postal clerks was an iron-barred partition, with an armed guard standing behind the bars. It reminded me of stories I had read of pawnshops in ancient China and trading posts in the early American West.

"Let's get out of here." I dragged my bewildered friend outside where the sun was bright and warm. The boys were still playing basketball. We climbed onto our bikes and rode home in half the time it had taken us to get there. Over dinner I warned my four roommates that, from then on, no one should go near that housing project. "We should avoid that street, especially the part near the project."

After that, we went to the downtown post office, though this was twice the distance. When we returned home from school late at night, we walked back along a safer but longer street. When Zhao got a notice for a registered letter, he asked the project post office if they could deliver it to our home so he wouldn't have to go to pick it up. The woman who received the call, a black woman herself, said she understood Zhao's situation perfectly. The area was not safe.

Half a year later, in an interview, I told a newspaper reporter that it seemed as if our black neighbors hated us

Chinese, and that I believed social welfare took away the dignity of poor people. In print the statements sounded racist. I should have made it clear that among people of any race and nationality there are good and bad; that we happened to live near a black housing project where there were a few bad youngsters; and that I had good black friends who wanted to help me understand the situation of their people.

I felt uneasy about this interview, and I was concerned about what my black friends would think of me. One black friend made the comment, "I was not happy reading what you said about blacks. But, at the same time, I am frustrated because I realize that you are telling the facts." I was particularly worried about offending one friend, a black woman on the faculty of a nursing school who had been a great help to me in Chicago. Fortunately, she was away in San Francisco when the article appeared in print. When she returned and asked to see the article, I told her I hadn't kept a copy. That was true; I felt guilty about the remarks I had made about blacks and didn't want to keep a copy around to remind me.

It took two months to build up enough courage for me to tell her about my remarks on American blacks. She understood. She said she was also cautious in certain black neighborhoods. The question, she said, is who is responsible for this? I was later to give a great deal of thought to that question.

Back in China in 1974, when I had read *Gone With the Wind*, I sympathized with Scarlett; I admired her courage and thought she was sensible in her treatment of black slaves. But a white American woman working in my office gave me a copy of *Jubilee*. "Read this, so you won't have such a one-sided view of American history," she said. *Jubilee* is a novel about how a slave family fought for its freedom and independence after the Civil War. I read it and afterward thought I then understood better the other point of view.

After a year in Chicago, where the population is 40 percent black, I was forced to see both sides. My sympathies went out to the inner-city poor blacks who lack an opportunity for a better education and, as a result, better job opportunities. My sympathies also went out to the middle-class people who are afraid, and who have to pay the taxes to support the social welfare system. I didn't like this kind of social welfare, not because people complained about paying for it, but because I believed it deprived the recipients of appreciating the value of an education and of work.

• • •

After I transferred to Circle, Dr. Liu gave me an office in his research center. I didn't have much to do there and so, after a week, I began to wander around the campus. Although I was associated with his research center, which belonged to the sociology department, I took only two sociology courses during my six quarters at Circle. I mainly took courses in the English department from two professors I came to know well through mutual friends. However, I maintained close contact with Dr. Liu. He invited me to his home so I could broaden my contacts with other people, drove me into the country to pick apples in the autumn, and took me out to the suburbs to see the tree leaves changing color, so I would feel less homesick.

But now that I was living with my Chinese friends, I found I had fewer opportunities to speak English. Even though the people all around me—in the streets, on buses and trains, and in the stores were speaking English—I couldn't seem to find a way to talk to them.

I remembered Victor's advice: be aggressive. One afternoon on my way home I stopped at an intersection to talk with an elderly lady who always helped schoolchildren cross the street. She was standing by herself on the corner. Since people are often talkative, I thought perhaps I could strike up a conversation with her. Unfortunately, she turned out to be hard of hearing, which only compounded the problem of my English. I left her to her job and walked down the street, nursing my loneliness. Along that same street a black man called out something to me. "No, pardon me?" I heard myself saying. Then the meaning of what he had said hit me—he was asking me for change for the parking meter. If I had understood him clearly, I would at least have been able to speak several sentences with him.

When I came to the parochial school on the corner, I saw a black boy playing inside behind the glass door, probably waiting for someone to pick him up. A young woman appeared in the doorway. On impulse I went up and knocked, and when she opened the door, I told her I was a journalist from China and was interested in talking to the principal. She let me in and led me to the principal's office. The principal, a kind-looking woman in her fifties, was sitting behind her desk. She and the two nuns with her were sealing envelopes. I went through my routine of self-introduction. With a notebook in hand, I pretended to be conducting an interview for my magazine, and this kind lady patiently answered all my questions. I told her something about Chinese elementary schools in order to stay longer.

As I emerged onto the street again, I felt good. At the same time my conscience bothered me. Was I too dishonest with this principal, telling her that I was interviewing her for a magazine? Should I have told her that I had sought her out just for a chance to speak English and an opportunity to get closer to American life? Such a trick would never work in China. There, every interview requires an official letter.

Lenin learned English by listening to soapbox orators in London's Hyde Park and by talking to people on the street. I would try to follow his example and look for these people along my way. On my way to and from school I often passed a white man, in his fifties, who was decently dressed and harmless looking. One day I saw him standing outside a small Polish restaurant, looking quite respectable in a clean, warm jacket and hat. He waved to me. I hailed him and stopped.

"How nice it is today," he said cheerfully, his nose and cheeks flushed."

It was a warm day in March and I was eager to talk. "I see you often. You don't live far from here, do you?" I asked.

"No, I live on the other side of Western Avenue," he answered with equal eagerness to start a conversation. "Where do you live?"

"Quite near. Well, I have to go now. I have a class at ten."

"Hey, young man, can you give me a dollar?" he called out to me. I suddenly realized that his looks had fooled me. Here, standing before me was a clean and well-dressed old man begging for money. Didn't he have sons or daughters? Why would they let him do this? I took out two quarters and handed them to him. "I'm sorry. I don't have a dollar," I said.

He was no different from the panhandlers I had seen on West Madison Street—Chicago's skid row. Margaret Shu, the Chinese-American nurse who lived on the second floor of our house, drove me through that street one day. It was not like other streets—litter was everywhere and the windows of most buildings were broken or boarded up. She pointed to the people on the sidewalk. "Most of them are drunks," she said. "They stand at the traffic lights and beg for money from car drivers when they stop. Did you lock the door?" I pushed down the button and rolled up the window.

"Do they work?" I was fascinated by these people—black, white, and Mexican—most of them in their fifties and sixties, and dressed shabbily and looking pathetic.

"They do odd jobs to earn enough to buy a fifth of whisky," she answered.

After that unpleasant encounter, I crossed the street whenever I saw the white man by the restaurant, pretending not to see him.

The need to speak English was so great I sometimes took foolish chances. One Saturday afternoon Yang came home looking agitated. "Four people grabbed me and took my money," he told us before he put down the box of detergent he had bought. "Luckily, I only had a dollar with me, so I gave it to them. I showed my pockets to them and they believed me."

"Where are they?" I asked.

"At the corner of Polk and Western."

"I'm going to see," I said.

"No," Yang and Zheng shouted in chorus. "You are not going. It's too dangerous."

"Don't worry, I can deal with them." Sounding bold is a sorry substitute for courage.

"Then I'll go with you," Yang said.

The four men who had robbed Yang were still there, standing in front of a tiny fast-food restaurant. At four o'clock in the afternoon the restaurant was doing a brisk business. Customers leaned against the window, eating their food out of paper sacks. Some of them seemed to know the four men, and were handing them food—hot dogs, French fries, and part of a hamburger.

The two blacks in the group were sitting on the sidewalk, leaning against the shop; a Mexican stood near the door; a fourth man, a white, leaned against a car, all of them eating the greasy carry-out food. I was struck by the ethnic mix of this group. It would have been perfect if I joined them as representative from the East. Yang lagged behind when he saw them, whispering to me, "That white man is the one who grabbed me and took my money."

The white man turned toward me as I approached. "Sir," he began, but his manner was not deferential, "Do you have any money?"

"I happen to need money, too, brother," I said. I took a step forward, trying my best to sound and look casual and unperterbed. I must take the initiative and overrule them, I was thinking. Here standing before me was a miserable white punk, too inept to be called a gangster. From the respectful manner of the other three, I figured he must be the leader. There is a Chinese saying: To capture the enemy you first subdue the chieftain. I put one hand on his shoulder and another on the lapel of his tattered suit. I shook the man and said, "Hey, brother, how about lending *me* some money?" I said it jokingly, putting on a smile that I hoped would thaw any hostility. "I am Chinese and I live nearby. Would you come and have a cup of Chinese tea with me? We may treat you to dinner, too." He looked down; my closeness was making him nervous. "My name is Liu. What's your name?"

"David," he grumbled. He turned and shouted "Jack!" to a black man. Jack got up from the curb and obediently came over, then stood waiting, obviously puzzled. "Give this gentleman some of your fries," David told him. If he doesn't eat, push them down his throat." He sounded fierce, but I thought he was only trying to save face.

Yang was standing ten feet away, frightened. I told him to go home, saying I would stay awhile with my new friends. He left. I took some fries from the greasy paper bag in Jack's dirty hand and ate them, anticipating a blow from David, but he didn't move.

"Give him more. He's starving," he said to Jack roughly.

Between bites, I asked him why he was demanding money from strangers in a country where the government provided social welfare. I had read in the newspaper that poor people under the poverty level were given rent support and food stamps every month. David told me he was a Vietnam veteran with five children. For three years he had been unemployed. The social relief was not enough to support his family.

"Do you drink?"

"No."

"Do you have any special skill?"

"No."

By now Yang had come back with Zheng Zhenyi. I told David I would like to talk to him again someday. He still looked fierce, but his tone was much less hostile. I then left with my two roommates.

"We were afraid they would hurt you so we brought twenty dollars to redeem you," Zheng Zhenyi said. He was not joking.

I laughed. "We had a very nice talk," I said. "Unfortunately my English was not good enough to communicate better. But next time, be sure to bring more money. I am worth more than twenty dollars!"

Actually I was scared by the encounter, and I had foolishly placed myself and my friends in danger. Every day the newspapers and television reported people being killed on the streets of Chicago. I might have thought I knew about American criminal activities, but all I really knew was what I had read in novels.

After that episode, I tended to avoid poor districts, public housing projects and the street hangouts of young unemployed youth. I never saw those four men again on Western, and there were now more police patrol cars in that area of the city.

For several years my family had lived on the edge of a rundown area of Beijing. Among my classmates were many children from low-income families. Through them I learned something about street gangs. I admired their daring deeds, and I loved to read stories about the outlaws of ancient times. Through a classmate I met one of the gang members, a strong, muscular and fiercely handsome boy. How I admired him! I wished I had a strong body like his so I could go with the street heroes and see how they lived. My body was built only for reading books and dreaming fantasies. After I learned English, I devoured Wild West stories, admiring the quickness of buffalo hunters, gamblers, gold miners, and sheriffs drawing their guns. I also thought I knew something about street gangs and gangsters and underground rules from reading *The Godfather*. I would sincerely like to meet some of the gangsters in the United

States. Maybe I could understand this part of America if the right person were to introduce me.

• • •

One Sunday, Zheng took me to Chicago's famous open market on Maxwell Street. The crowds were so dense that we could not walk through them very fast. Cars crawled bumper to bumper, inch by inch. Absorbed in their shopping, people moved from one cardboard stand to the next, examining a jacket here or a pair of pants there. Shoes, old and new, were dumped in boxes or displayed on stands. A peddler shouted loudly about his T-shirts and sweaters, new ones with brand names, apparently taken from overstocked warehouses or unsuspecting trucks. A Japanese had a stand selling stereos, a Korean couple sold synthetic leather suitcases, and Indians sold exotic-looking statues and ornaments. Old clothes were displayed on racks along walls, piled on tables, and thrown over the tops of wagons that had brought these peddlers and their goods to this place from the west and south sides of Chicago.

I had already read Berkow's *Maxwell Street*, a book on the history of this open market established by the first Jewish settlers one hundred years ago. As they became rich and moved away, Polish peddlers, then blacks, and now primarily Latinos, replaced them. The marketplace was littered and dirty, as it always had been, according to the book: garbage on the ground, filthy rags, fruit rinds, and urine-smelling garbage burning in big dark trash drums.

There had been changes, though. No longer were there any squawking live chickens, live fish, butcher shops, or peddlers dragging customers to their stands. The hot dog stand was still as busy as it was, no doubt, a hundred years ago. But trucks and wagons had replaced push-carts and many customers arrived in cars, though old models of shabby appearance. There may have been pickpockets, but I saw none of the brutal fights or prostitutes openly soliciting, as described in Berkow's book. The only people I was afraid to get involved with were watch sellers. My first experience with one left a deep impression.

Zheng and I were strolling from one stand to another, wondering why, in the middle of such a rich city, there could be a place like Maxwell Street where people sold old shoes and torn pants when a black man in his early thirties came up to us. Stretching out his hand, he showed me a watch. "Do you want this watch?" he said in a friendly way.

"How much?" I stupidly thought I might have a conversation with him.

"A hundred dollars." The sticker on the watch said $195. A good bargain, I thought.

"No," I said. I didn't want to buy a watch yet.

"OK, how about $60?"

"What?" I was taken aback. "Only $60 for a $195 watch?" I couldn't believe it, and my suspicions were aroused. "No, I don't have much money with me," I said in haste and tried to get away.

"How much do you have?" He appeared very sympathetic. "Thirty? Twenty-five?"

I began to regret that I had let him know I could speak English. "No I don't want it," I said, and escaped with my friend.

The next time I visited Maxwell Street I didn't hesitate to say no to watch pushers. However, I later did buy a used bicycle and a typewriter there for $15 each.

Maxwell Street may not have been a shocking experience for mainland Chinese, but it definitely was a thing beyond our wildest imagination. In spite of all published reports in China that some Americans are poor and starving, it is assumed, particularly by the young, that the United States is a place of unlimited wealth. I didn't even expect to find second-hand-clothing shops in Chicago. By seeing what was sold on Maxwell street, I learned that not all Americans throw away shirts after three washings, as Beijing sanitation workers have reported American diplomats did with their clothes.

When the weather turned warm I went several times to Maxwell Street not to buy, but to enjoy the free blues music that I soon came to love. The entertainers performed in a small opening behind the bustling cardboard stands. They dressed plainly—some poorly—and performed songs with great sincerity. Spectators swayed and tapped their feet to the rhythms. One day, perhaps some of these street musicians may become famous.

In a way I liked Maxwell Street. It brought to mind the open markets in old Beijing, a reminder of the times when people felt much freer and easier with life. And it was a distinct contrast to the rigid, electronic life along Chicago's affluent Michigan Avenue.

CHAPTER SEVEN

CHICAGO RICH AND POOR

The common frustration expressed by all four staff members of *China Reconstructs*, studying in the United States, was our difficulty in talking to Americans. Later in the year, when two of these staff members came to Chicago for their 1981 winter vacation, they were surprised to find that I had a number of American friends. "You are the only one of us in the United States who has so many social contacts," they said with envy, but I explained to them how much mental struggle I had gone through before I developed these friends. I had advantages over them because I was staying in Chicago, a cosmopolitan community where there are social activities going on all the time. My three colleagues were staying in small college towns where most people's interests are academic.

Before I left Beijing, Ron Dorfman gave me two neatly typed sheets of paper. "Here's a list of people you can call," he said. "They're all good friends. Just say I told you to call, and suggest getting together for a drink or lunch." There were twenty-two names on the sheets, with addresses and telephone numbers. At the bottom of the second page he had written: "This ought to keep you busy until I get there. Have fun."

I wasn't having fun, and the two sheets stayed in my traveling bag for four months. Many times I took the list and read it from top to bottom, looking for a name that might sound "friendly." And each time I put it back in the bag again. My hesitation came from the fear of being refused. How would these people who had never met me react to my call? All of them were writers, doctors, or lawyers. If I called, would they feel they had to see me so as not to offend Ron?—in that case, I would be a burden to them. Or, what if they didn't want to see me at all? I would lose face. That was the last thing in the world I wanted.

I am not a gregarious person and I'm not very interested in social activities. In China, though I have many friends, I rarely visited them in their homes. On major holidays I felt obliged to pay half-day visits to my father's and my father-in-law's family, but I was not even good at socializing with my own relatives. In the United States, however, I would learn nothing if I didn't meet people.

"You're such a timid stick-in-the-mud, it's almost beyond belief," Ron later wrote in one of his letters. "Call Al and tell him you'd like to go to Riccardo's Restaurant on Friday night. Ask him to introduce you around. Call Irene and tell her you'd like to try some Chinese restaurants with her and Don and Nancy. Call Steve Gittelson at *Chicago Magazine* and tell him you'd like to come down and take a look at the magazine's operations. Same with Mike Minor at the *Reader*, and Laura Green at the *Chicago Sun-Times*..."

I finally gathered enough courage to call Mike Minor. The comments on Ron's list under Mike's name read as follows: "He's one of the best writers in Chicago. He works two days a week at the *Reader*, a weekly newspaper, as a copy editor. His wife, Betsy Nore, is a specialist in teaching English as a second language. She also owns a clothing store. Mike is a Vietnam war veteran who returned to Vietnam as a reporter to write about the fall of Saigon." I called him and he invited me to dinner at his house. I was comfortable with the Minors, both my age, who treated me as a respected friend.

At their house, I met Eliot, a reporter for the *Chicago Sun-Times*, who offered to give me a tour of the office of this daily newspaper. I readily accepted, feeling rewarded for almost the first time since I had come to the United States. I was deeply impressed by the tour of the *Sun-Times* offices. I was mostly fascinated by their word processors. On every reporter's and editor's desk was a terminal. Eliot sat down before one and demonstrated how it worked. In my office we were still using manual typewriters made in the late 1940s, models of which I saw on display in a museum in Washington, D.C.; our two Italian-made electric typewriters broke down so often, no one in the office dared to touch them anymore. If I can save enough money while I am in the United States, I will take a word processor back, I dreamed as I listened to Eliot explain the magic apparatus. The printing presses of the *Sun-Times* were not so impressive. We had a better one in our printing house in Beijing.

A month later Mike took me to a blues concert at the Blackstone Hotel. The songs bored me before long, but I didn't want to say anything because I didn't want to hurt Mike's feelings. I don't know if he saw my indifferent expression or was bored, too, but he suggested that we leave after less than an hour. In that tiny concert hall, blacks, dressed in very expensive clothes, composed two-thirds of the audience; it seemed that I was gradually coming into contact with authentic American culture.

As the days got warmer, I became more and more active. With greater confidence in my English, I struck out in all directions: I visited the homes of people active in the U.S.-China People's Friendship Association, and I went to some parties given by Ron's friends. At a luncheon I met Iris Shannon, a black woman and an associate professor of community health nursing at Rush-Presbyterian-St. Luke's Medical Center in Chicago. She was conducting a course for her students on medical care in China and asked me to be her class resource person.

Unlike Chinese universities in which the school authorities decide what courses should be offered, American universities give their professors a much greater voice in curriculum. The fact that a course on Chinese medical care was being taught in a college of nursing amazed me—what would American nurses do with such knowledge? Western medical care is much more advanced than that of China.

Through the spring quarter four students attended Iris's class. She showed slides of Chinese hospitals and sanatoriums, and talked about barefoot doctors, preventive medicine, and birth control policies that allow women who give birth two paid months of maternity leave. I enthusiastically told the small audience what I knew about such subjects. I felt good, realizing that I knew a little about everything; my editor once said I would make a good journalist for this reason.

I also took advantage of this class to practice my English. Iris later took me along when she was invited to lecture to the nursing staff of another hospital. A pretty black nurse in the audience told me I spoke very good English—I was never so happy. At the end of the quarter, Iris and her students entertained me with a dinner as a gesture of thanks.

Iris was proud of her black origins. One day in August, she drove me for four hours around the various neighborhoods of Chicago's west and south sides. The first place we stopped was a black neighborhood health center in a poor district. On the streets outside, young men and women were standing in front of shops and on corners, drinking and smoking; it was Wednesday. "They don't have jobs," Iris said sadly.

I was impressed by the neat, clean wards and

well-mannered staff of the health center. A friend of Iris's who served as our guide told me that after three years the health center had become self-sufficient and no longer needed to receive government funding. Almost all the staff and patients were black. During our more than one-hour tour, I saw only half a dozen Mexican patients and two or three white staff members. In a corner on the second floor I saw several 9-inch television sets on a semi-circular counter, behind which two uniformed guards were chatting, pistols at their waists.

"What are the TVs for?" I asked our guide.

"They are monitoring the vicinity around the hospital." On the screen I saw the parking lot where Iris had parked her car.

I mentioned that I would like to come to work for a day or two as a volunteer; the guide smiled and said, half seriously, half jokingly, "you'd better give me a call before you come. People here are suspicious of outsiders."

From the health center we drove south on the Dan Ryan Expressway. The car bumped along, hitting potholes, despite Iris's careful maneuvering. The buildings on each side of the expressway looked shabby; grass grew wild on the slopes. After we passed 80th Street, the scene began to brighten. We drove through several white neighborhoods, where the houses were better taken care of than those around 34th Street. We then drove to "Pill Hill," a neighborhood where many black doctors live. The houses were no less elegant than those along Sheridan Road in Evanston, though they were more modern.

Not far from Pill Hill was Beverly Hills, where the houses are surrounded by large lawns and brightly painted fences. Unseen birds chirped happily among thick bushes on the lawns. Even though it was August, the surroundings looked cool. A group of white high school students walked along the sidewalk in the tree shade. "This area is predominately upper-middle class white," Iris said, seeing my curiosity. The quality of the children's clothes was as obvious as was their breeding. The contrast between rich and poor in Chicago was striking, and the racial segregation was distinctive.

Iris took me to her own house on 83rd Street on the far south side of Chicago, a very pleasant neighborhood, housing members of the black middle class. The street was tranquil and clean and the houses, though not as overwhelming as those in Evanston, were neat and comfortable. Her husband, Robert, was meticulously mowing the lawn when we arrived. He came over and greeeted me warmly. Iris was glad to show me her tastefully decorated home, and Robert treated me to the best barbecued ribs I had ever had.

Another summer day a friend of mine drove me from Logan Square on the northwest side of Chicago to a party in Hyde Park on the southeast side. On our way we passed through neighborhoods of different nationalities. In a park I saw three groups having picnics; from their skin color and clothing I could tell that one group was Mexican, another Puerto Rican, and the third, black. Although it was not a big park, the three groups kept strictly to themselves. The asphalt paths of the park served as boundaries dividing these three grass-lot nations.

On another occasion I went to a dinner at the house of T.T. Chen, an active member of the U.S.-China People's Friendship Association. I emerged from the subway station on the way to his house on the northwest side of Chicago and found I was lost. I asked two middle-aged men at a bus stop for directions; they shook their heads. I thought my English was not understood and repeated the question. They shook their heads again, this time uttering some unintelligible sounds. I asked two others; they couldn't understand me, either. Finally two boys roller-skating in the street took me to T.T. Chen's house. One of them explained to me that this was a Polish immigrant neighborhood; many of the Poles had lived there for thirty or forty years and had never learned to speak English.

As my American friends drove me around the city they always mentioned the racial and/or ethnic makeup of the people living in each area. Chicago, an international city, can be divided into pockets of Polish, Jewish, Mexican, Greek, Puerto Rican, and many other peoples. I could see the change in the ethnic and racial composition of Chicagoans whenever I rode the No. 49 bus along Western Avenue, the longest thoroughfare in Chicago. Going from north to south, I could not help noticing the changes in skin color of the boarding passengers—from whites to dark-skinned Latinos to blacks, with a mixture of yellows as we passed through the Chinatown area. I hated the No. 49 bus, not only because it was too slow—thirty minutes between runs—but because I didn't feel safe riding it.

One Sunday in summer 1981 a friend and I were heading for a discount department store far to the north on Western Avenue. We got on the bus at Polk Street; more than half of the passengers already seated were Mexicans. Several blocks north, blacks crowded on. After a few more stops, some whites entered. Whether whites, blacks or Mexicans, I could tell from their clothes and manner that none of them were rich people. Of course, I thought, only poor people use public transportation. Rich people don't wait at bus stops for half an hour; their time is worth more money than poor people's.

At Jackson Boulevard, an angry middle-aged black man got on the bus. He waved a crumpled transfer in front of the driver, whose eyes were more on the passenger's face than on the ticket. The black man stalked to the rear of the bus. I turned my head away from the window, stealing side-glances at the newcomer. "There might be trouble," my friend whispered. "We'd better get off and take the next bus." I nodded my head in silence.

The next thing I heard was a Mexican woman screaming and a Mexican man shouting. This couple had been sitting, talking quietly in the last row. Now the black man was hitting the Mexican man and the Mexican woman was pleading, tears running down her face. The bus was two-thirds full, yet no one intervened. Most of the passengers were looking at the scene with no emotion on their faces. The Mexican woman managed to pull her companion away from the fighting and lead him to a seat near the driver, who continued driving as if nothing had happened.

The shirt of the Mexican man was torn, revealing bloody scratches on his chest; his face was flushed with anger and excitement. The woman spoke soothingly to him in Spanish and looked timidly toward the rear. The black man was now quiet. We got off the moment the driver opened the door. From then on, I avoided the No. 49 and most other Chicago buses, unless I had to take one in an emergency.

Every day, on the way to the Circle campus, I bicycled through a small park where young people played baseball and children from an elementary school across the street did exercises. During school recess, the races mingled, but after class they dispersed into groups according to skin color. I never saw young people of different colors voluntarily playing together, even when two or three groups were using the same playground.

There are two rivers in central China that meet at a certain point. Their two courses join, but their two waters don't merge. The clear water of the Jing stays on one side of the river; the muddy water of the Wei on the other. From this, the Chinese have a saying: "As clear-cut as the waters of the Jing and Wei rivers." The situation among the races in Chicago is like these two rivers, or so it seems to me.

In May 1981, at a U.S.-China People's Friendship Association conference, I met Barbara Butz. She was editing the association newsletter and asked me to write something for it. I wrote a short piece about watching American TV, but because the organization was short on publishing funds, it never came out in print. However, I found a real friend in Barbara.

• • •

A social-work administrator, Barbara participated in a volunteer tutoring program of the U.S.-China Friendship Association to aid visiting Chinese scholars in learning English. Her Chinese student was a woman studying at Northwestern University, and Barbara wanted me to meet her.

Three times during that summer Barbara invited me, the Chinese woman, and one of my roommates to her father's house on North Sheridan Road in Glencoe. As we were driving there on our first visit, I became aware of the fact that from Evanston north, I had seen only white people. The only dark faces here were white ones tanned by the sun; the only oriental faces were those of we three Chinese. We stopped at a grocery store in Winnetka, a suburb north of Evanston, to buy some food. Out of habit, I began to roll up the car window; Barbara gestured for me to leave it open. "That's not necessary here," she assured me. We didn't even have to lock the car, and to test the safety of this place, I left my camera on the car seat while we went into the store; it remained untouched.

In Chicago reports of burgleries and robberies were constantly in newspapers and on TV news programs. Zhao Jian, my roommate, left his year-old, not-very-fancy bicycle in front of a building on the university campus for less than an hour; its lock was broken and the bicycle was stolen. Another group of Chinese made the mistake of leaving two pairs of pants near an open window of their apartment overnight. On Chicago's west side, one dared not leave a car on the street unlocked for even a minute. Here in Winnetka, people didn't bother to lock their cars.

I didn't see any police cars or hear sirens screaming, as I often did on Western Avenue. I did see one car with "Community Security" lettered discreetly on its side. Its operators, two young policemen in short-sleeved uniforms that were far less provoking than the blue uniforms of the Chicago city police, were chatting under the shade of a tree; they didn't carry pistols or sticks. All was quiet; a few children were playing together near a sidewalk and there was no sound of car horns. Here, cars weren't disfigured with rust and could be driven without having to dodge potholes. How nice it must be to be rich! The well-kept roads, immense lawns and mansions surrounded by trees and gardens were beyond anything I could have imagined—even a Chinese minister of state wouldn't have such a magnificent dwelling.

Barbara's friend pointed to a car parked in front of a great mansion and told me it was worth $500,000—I could hardly believe my ears. She said it was a Roll-Royce, entirely handmade. When a person has more money than he can spend, he buys things for showing off, I thought. We passed a country club which they told me has a membership fee of $500 a year. It seemed a great deal to pay just for the use of its swimming pool; later I learned that some people pay much more for club memberships.

Barbara's father, Herbert Butz, was nowhere in sight when we arrived. Barbara ushered us in through the unlocked kitchen door—again I expressed surprise at this lack of concern for security. Barbara's friend told me there was no theft problem in Glencoe. I was unable to comprehend this until Barbara said her father paid $1,300 each year for property tax and public services. People who could afford to live here certainly would not steal, and those who might drive from the south or west sides of Chicago to steal would be easily recognized as outsiders.

On Sunday Barbara took us to Ravinia Park where we had a picnic on the lawn before the Chicago Symphony began its 8:00 P.M. performance. Ravinia is a 36-acre park near the south end of the town of Highland Park. Its pavilion has very high calibre acoustics and three thousand seats for outdoor concerts. When the symphony orchestra plays, the music can be heard anywhere in the park over an electronic sound system. We listened from the grass with an overlooking view of the amphitheater; fifteen dollars for a ticket to sit inside the theater was too much to pay and, besides, listening on the grass with candlelight and wine was much more fun.

On the second visit to Glencoe, we rode bicycles through a forest preserve. It was a large area divided by the winding Chicago River, with trees that were thick and immense. Every time I was in a place like this I could not help marveling at how Americans are able to keep such wild beauty right on the edge of a big city. Here we were, forty miles from downtown Chicago, in a large forest. In woods like these I was totally relaxed, sometimes thinking about how good it would be if Fengyun and our son could be enjoying it with me.

During the years I have lived in Beijing, the population of the city has tripled. It has become very crowded; the parks within the city limits which used to be places for city dwellers to relax are now small patches of grass enclosed by fences and guarded by park administrators; parks in the suburbs that used to be quiet are no longer so. Fragrance Hill Park rarely had visitors when I was studying English and living near there from 1965 to 1968. Now it has tens of thousands of visitors every day—hundreds of buses and cars bringing these visitors line up at the entrance gate when the autumn leaves turn red. It is hard to find a quiet place in Beijing on Sundays.

Barbara's father took me out onto Lake Michigan in his sailboat and taught me the basic rules of sailing. Several dozen boats, with sails or motors, were skipping over wind-ruffled water; many of the occupants were young lovers. The lake stretched out to the horizon and the sand on the shore was pure and inviting for swimmers. How marvelous this place would be if it were in China! Selfishly I wished I had that magic lantern that might transport it there.

One Saturday, at my request, Barbara drove me to see the

Dwight Correctional Center, a women's prison ninety miles south of Chicago. We left early in the morning in a drizzling rain and encountered few cars on the highway. It was pleasan', looking at the green fields of corn and beans, shrouded in a rainy haze. We passed dozens of bungalows and Victorian-style homes. Barbara told me that the people who owned those homes worked in the city of Chicago. They drove one hour each way to and from the metropolis in order to go to work.

A large shopping center standing in the middle of a field caught my eye. "Who comes here to buy things?" I wondered aloud.

"People drive here from the city," Barbara said. I didn't ask why they drove to this out-of-the-way place to shop, but I could imagine this large, elegant shopping center becoming a ghost town if the city ever ran out of gas.

We stopped at a service station to ask directions. In front of us, a shabby car with a middle-aged black man and two black women inside was pulling out of the station. Barbara said, "They must be going to Dwight, too."

The attendant said yes, for us to follow the car, that it was going to Dwight.

When we arrived, I couldn't believe at first that what I saw was a prison. All around were neat lawns, flowerbeds, and seven or eight two-story Victorian houses standing apart and linked by cement paths. Chipmunks and squirrels played on the grass, and green fields stretched out in all directions. It was quite peaceful. If somebody had told me that this was a summer resort for wealthy people, I would have readily accepted the statement. The only thing that reminded me of the prison life I once knew was double-barred doors.

The warden, a delicate-looking young woman of twenty-seven who could have easily been mistaken for a Michigan Avenue shopper, conducted our tour. She had a master key that fit every door. The guards were locked inside with the inmates, for their own safety. If the guards don't have keys, the warden explained, the inmates won't attack them to get those keys.

I saw three middle-aged women in a dayroom playing cards. A 25-inch color television was turned on, but nobody was watching. Upstairs were bedrooms, each shared by two or three persons, with a small TV set on in every room.

In one room I noticed a kitchen. "Are they allowed to cook?" I asked. "Yes," the warden replied, "but the food cooked in rooms must be provided by families or friends outside." She explained that regular meals are served in the cafeteria, where both the inmates and staff eat.

We went to the cafeteria, where guards and prisoners alike waited in line to buy food from the same counter. I was impressed; in most parts of the world, prison food is a form of punishment.

I didn't see any barbed wire or armed guards. "Have you ever had jailbreaks?" I asked. "No," the warden answered. "We have a very sophisticated communications system. When an inmate leaves her group to go to another place, that person's guard notifies another guard that she is going through the C.R. system. If the inmate has not shown up within twenty minutes, an alarm system is activated. Patrol cars are then sent out to search for the prisoner. The prison is five miles from any community or public transportation, so it is nearly impossible to escape."

The warden told me the state government spends more than $6 million a year on the current inmate population of 345, averaging $18 thousand per prisoner. "That's more than the prisoners could make working outside," I remarked.

"Yes," she said. "The government spends more on them than it pays most of our guards."

Sixty-seven percent of the Dwight prison population was black, and more than 80 percent came from Chicago's poor areas. According to the warden, the projected population would be 600 by 1985. That meant a larger budget for prisons, despite other pressing needs for public money. I wondered why the government didn't spend more money on children and less on prisoners. It seemed to me that if poor people got a better education, the rate of crime would go down.

As we drove away, I looked back at this "hotel" prison. The rain was still falling; several women visitors were coming out of a small building where inmates could be visited by their families; some of the young children were weeping; others were laughing and shouting. On our way back to Chicago, Barbara talked about organizing a citizens' group to help these imprisoned mothers.

On another occasion I and two Chinese colleagues visited the Juvenile Detention Center located near my residence. It was a large concrete and steel building, the inside spotless. On the second floor along a corridor were single rooms, each with one bed, which looked warm and comfortable. One separate section was set aside for the school. Our guide, a security staff member, turned us over to the school principal.

"This school is run by the Chicago Board of Education so it is not under the jurisdiction of the court," the principal told us. I was fascinated; in China we also have such schools, but they are under the administration of the police. The principal was glad to have Chinese visitors because he had been in China. In many places I met Americans who had been to China.

Some children were sitting in classrooms. They behaved politely, looking at us with curious smiles. The principal showed us the kitchen where the young delinquents could learn to cook, and a workshop where a dozen boys, thirteen to fifteen years of age, were learning to mold figures from clay. Their work was so simple that any Chinese elementary school pupil could have done it.

Sometime later, while talking with a black judge, I said that the Chinese practice of dealing with juvenile delinquents was better than in America. In America, the courts, police, and city government are separated from each other; in China, they cooperate closely. The parents are also kept informed about their children's behavior in prison. That, I told the judge, is one reason for the lower crime rate in China.

Again and again, I concluded that the American government invests too much in the prison system. I joked with the security officer on our way out of the detention center, saying that it must be a better place than the homes of these young kids.

"It sure is," the officer said with a smile.

CHAPTER EIGHT

COLLEGE LIFE

I n August 1981, Ran Xiancuy came from China to attend Illinois State University in the town of Normal on an exchange program with Beijing's Foreign Languages Press, of which *China Reconstructs* is a part. This program started in 1980, and Ran and her three colleagues made up the second group to come. I was glad Ran had gotten the chance to study in the United States, and was happy her stay coincided with mine.

Ran had taken, but failed, the same government scholarship examination I had taken. I admired her gracious handling of this failure; I had really expected that she would be jealous or would find excuses to belittle me. At the time she graduated from the prestigious Beijing Foreign Languages Institute, in 1966, I had learned just enough English to struggle through abridged novels. She was hired by *China Reconstructs* in 1968 as a translator. By 1978, she was recognized by everyone on the staff as a very competent translator. My "talents" were appreciated only by a couple of veteran colleagues. Some of the staff members felt righteously indignant about the outcome of our examinations: how could a country boy like Liu Zongren, without a college education, have succeeded? Ran was disappointed, but didn't change her attitude toward me, despite the fact that she had wanted the chance badly.

Shortly before I left China, I found her alone one afternoon in the office. After telling me to watch my loose tongue—I often got into trouble for being too outspoken—she hesitantly mentioned that one of her schoolmates had gone to the United States and was working there in order to pay for studies at the university. Immediately I understood what she was trying to convey. I hoped I might be able to find such a work-study opportunity for her.

After I had been in Evanston for two months, I wrote to her and, in a roundabout way, hinted that she wouldn't be happy coming to the United States on such a program. True, I was paid by the Chinese government, but I still found it difficult to get along. She didn't mention this matter in later letters to me, but I knew that she still hoped to come to the United States by any means possible. It is not easy to convince those Chinese who have even the slightest hope of going abroad to study that life in a foreign land can be very difficult. When Ran wrote me that she was coming on the exchange program, I felt strangely relieved of my responsibility to her.

She and the others had been in Normal for only two weeks when Ron Dorfman, who was now back in Chicago, and I drove to see them. Summer vacation was coming to an end and their dormitory was bustling with returning students. Tan Aiqing, another woman from *China Reconstructs*, agreed to join Ran and the two of us after Ron suggested going out for a drink. As we walked out of the dorm, I asked Ran how she was feeling about her stay in the United States. Tears welled up in her eyes. "Now you understand what it means to go abroad alone," I said half jokingly. "You will feel better after school begins. Remember that you only have nine months to stay here. I still have more than a year to go."

Normal, like Evanston, was too quiet a community to enable much learning about American culture. It took only a few minutes for Ron to drive us around the entire university town. We stopped in a bar and reminisced over a glass of beer. At about nine in the evening, we went back to the dormitory, where a dance was being held; that made our reunion a little livelier.

At midnight, Ron and I left for the three-hour drive back to Chicago. The night air was cool and refreshing. My mind was occupied by one question: why do we Chinese want to leave our families behind for such long and miserable periods of stay in a foreign country?

At Christmastime, Ran and Tan came to Chicago for their winter vacation. I was determined to make their stay worthwhile. I asked several American friends for help; they assured me they would be glad to do something for my colleagues. Christmas is a time of parties, and Ron Dorfman and I arranged a schedule so full of activities that Tan and Ran finally had to refuse any more invitations. They were envious of the fact that I had so many friends in Chicago. "We have nowhere to go in Normal," Tan complained. "Every day we go to class and come back to our dorm. In the evening we watch television. I have learned as much during the three-week stay in Chicago as I have absorbed in five months in Normal. No wonder your English has improved so quickly."

They compared their life in Normal to times during China's bitter Cultural Revolution, when many Chinese city office workers were required to work on farms so as to receive "education through manual labor." "All around us are only fields," they said, complaining about the location of their school.

I had my pain, too. It hurt my pride to be so dependent on my American friends. I told my colleagues that my life was not always so full. Most of the time my life was like theirs.

Since I didn't want to trouble my American friends, I seldom took the initiative to get in touch with them, and only went out to see them when they asked me. I was not sure I convinced them because, after they returned to Normal, Tan wrote me saying she was impressed by my wide social contacts. If they had only known, they would have realized that I often felt just as isolated and rejected as they did.

• • •

In China, teacher-student relationships have a long tradition of being as important as that between a father and his son. At Medill I had found the relationship between students and professors rigid; they had little to do with one another outside the classroom. At Circle I felt the students behaved too freely in the classroom. They drank coffee and ate food in class, and put their feet on the desks in front of them. Nevertheless, I did like the way classes were conducted and how students were encouraged to take part in class discussions. At first I thought the professors might not be well prepared and therefore didn't have much to say. But later I learned that through debate and discussion the students are encouraged to develop independent thinking.

I really didn't need to take classes at Circle campus in order to learn about American culture. Speeches, rallies and free entertainment in the city, and extracurricular activities on the campus, were more than enough to educate me. Whenever I went to the center of the city I would spend an hour or so at the Daley Center Plaza or at the First National Plaza, where I listened to a black band or a brass concert, watched a dance group perform, or listened to a group of singers. Sometimes I went to the lake shore to watch people fishing and to strike up a casual conversation with one or two fishermen. Chicagoans are generally friendly and outgoing. Someone told me if I had been in New York I wouldn't have made so many friends.

There were always events going on at the Chicago Circle

Center (the students called it the "CCC"), a seven-story campus building with meeting rooms, rest rooms, lounges, adjoining recreation center, and several cafeterias. This center provided a stage on which the whole drama of American college life was played. I often smelled marijuana in the lounge there, where I liked to sit between classes so that I might listen to students talk in various accents. There were meetings and events staged to promote every kind of political idea—right and left, and neutral—and almost every kind of religion. One day I saw several American Hindu monks chanting prayers there, looking out-of-place in their yellow robes because of their fair skin, blue eyes and high noses. There were also army, navy, and airforce men who distributed pamphlets to the students showing how many benefits a student might receive by joining the armed forces. When the weather was good, many of these activities were moved out of the center and onto the campus lawn.

Every Monday I checked the campus newspaper, which had a calendar listing of all events, and I marked those of interest. I went to speeches and lectures by right or left-wing speakers, trying not to become involved. One day a group demonstrated in support of President Reagan's policy toward El Salvador. Three Central American students shouted at them and an argument ensued. Another day a group demonstrated against Reagan's aid to El Salvador. There were also a few hoots. An American friend told me that in the 1960s the campus was much more politically active than it was now.

One group on campus, calling itself the Gay and Lesbian Illini, met every week. I was enormously curious about this group which concerned itself with issues of homosexuality, but I never ventured to go to any of their meetings. I inquired of friends, however, to find out who these people were and what they did.

One of my friends argued that love between those of the same sex is natural and has existed throughout history—

during the Roman Empire, it was even made legal, he said. I disagreed, saying that it wouldn't be good for society to open up this issue. In old China, homosexuality was practiced by a few rich people, but the general public didn't approve. Neither of our arguments was especially supportable so we dropped the subject. Later I met a couple of homosexuals. They seemed to be decent people who held decent jobs. Their image was not so strange to me anymore, but their gay life was still a mystery.

During my first quarter at Circle I had taken two courses, one on the industrial countries of East Asia and the other, a laboratory course at the Speech and Hearing Clinic. I took the one on industrial relations not because I was interested in the subject, but because I thought I would feel comfortable with Professor Dick Barrett, to whom I had been introduced by Dr. Liu. I liked Professor Barrett. Young and broadly read, he often plied me with questions about China. I frequently went to his office to talk and occasionally I had lunch with him.

I met Kan, a Japanese student, in this industrial relations class. Kan always came in two minutes after the class had begun and Professor Barrett had already started drawing graphs on the two blackboards. Barrett used the blackboards to their full potential in his one-and-a-half-hour lecture. Kan would enter, walk to the chair next to me and sit down soundlessly. One day after class I introduced myself to Kan, and we went to the cafeteria together, where he bought a sandwich and a cup of coffee from the vending machine for his supper. I bought only a cup of coffee; I would have a Chinese dinner later at home. For two hours we stayed in the cafeteria talking.

Kan's English was no better than mine, but we had a nice conversation exploring information about each other's countries. He was alone in the United States, working half-time to support himself so that he could get a master's degree in business management. I never could understand why he came to the United States to learn management when so many American companies now go to Japan to find their management consultants. Kan and I went to the cafeteria to talk after class every Thursday evening for the rest of the semester. Though we were from different countries and different cultures, we were both from the Far East and were both lonely.

The other course I took in my first semester at Circle, at the Speech and Hearing Clinic, was not a formal course, but an informal one. Yet it taught me more about American culture than any of the formal sessions. What I learned there was a major factor in my being able to adjust to the complexities of American society, and much of the credit for my progress must go to the thoughtful guidance and encouragement of Professor Judy Curry, the director of the Clinic.

I first met her before I transferred to Circle from Medill. My friends at Circle, Zheng Zhenyi and Zhao Jian, talked about Judy, telling me how kind she was and how she had helped them in many ways. She turned out to be the bridge person I needed to close the gap between the culture of China and that of the United States.

After I transferred to Circle, Judy arranged to talk to me once a week so as to help improve my conversational English and correct my pronunciation. For my textbook, she assigned articles from newspapers and magazines. I read them beforehand and then discussed them with her in our one-hour sessions. She or her assistant made tapes of the words or sentences I had difficulty with so that I could practice them in the language laboratory.

Judy was not only a good teacher but also my personal counselor. I went to her for advice on many problems, and asked her to correct articles I wrote for practice or for publication. She entertained me and my collegues when they visited Chicago. I even asked her about everyday practical problems, such as what to do after I found I had been overcharged on a purchase at a store.

"There won't be a problem," she said on the phone. "Tomorrow morning you go there. Do you have the receipt? You do, good. Take it with you and explain to the salesman. He will refund your money. Do you want me to go with you? Are you sure? OK. If you have any trouble, call me at my office. Good."

With Judy's advice I went back to the store and was able to get my money back. But without her telling me how to handle that situation, I don't know what might have happened; I probably would have lost my thirty dollars, and might have gotten into trouble when I complained.

Another person I came to know at the Speech and Hearing Clinic was Mary Ann, the office secretary. Six feet tall and heavyset, she looked younger than her age of thirty-eight. She had once been the manager of a store and was not very used to taking orders from others, but she worked diligently and was meticulous with the annoying papers and files at the office.

"I like to talk to people I like," she said one day when I dropped in, as I often did, without an appointment. "I like you. We have a lot in common."

I liked her, too. Both of us were critical of people who were too ambitious and greedy, but both of us worked hard in the hope of improving ourselves. She told me about her family and I told her about mine, including some intimate details I wouldn't have told anyone else, least of all an American woman.

In 1982 the slow economy forced the university to cut some programs and reduce its staff, including some of the staff at the Speech and Hearing Clinic. Mary Ann and a speech therapist were told their jobs were ending in August, and they were not happy. I hated to see Mary Ann lose her job, although, perhaps, it was not as satisfactory to her as she might have wished. But losing a job is very different from quitting one, and she was worried about being able to find another one. I was not used to this kind of change. I felt lucky that I had a safe job back in China.

To give me more practice in conversational English, the Speech and Hearing Clinic assigned Jean, a student of social work, to work with me for another hour each week. Jean was one of the part-time instructors in a special program, called Cross Cultural Communication Skills, established for foreign students on the campus. The instructors were to conduct their hourly sessions in a different setting each week, settings which required different communications strategies. Jean was a person who enjoyed almost every setting. Her students might find themselves one week in a bowling alley, the next in the library, and the third week in one of the small laboratory rooms in the Speech and Hearing Clinic. She asked me how I wanted to proceed with our sessions. Before I could think of anything, she suggested that we go somewhere else to talk. I didn't object; though young, she was, after all, the teacher.

For our first meeting, Jean taught me to play pool at the Circle campus recreation center. Her purpose was to teach me the vocabulary of this game. At the second session we went to a college bar on Taylor Street, just west of the campus. Ron and some other friends had taken me to several restaurants and high-class bars to try different ethnic foods and exotic drinks, but I had not yet been to a "typical" side-street campus bar. Such places looked so dark from the outside that I suspected something sinister had to be going on inside. But I did want to know what an American bar was really like, and so Jean took me to one. We went a little after five in the afternoon. "This is called 'Happy Hour'," she explained, as if giving a lecture. "After five, beer sells at a lower price and then you will see a lot of students in the bar."

The few professors and other customers there looked different from those in the bars on Rush Street where Ron had taken me one night. Here people dressed casually and were quiet and well-behaved, quite the opposite from the wild images I had conjured up from reading American novels about knife fights, killings, prostitution and gambling in bars. We each had a cold beer and talked in almost a whisper.

Ron once asked me why I hadn't taken him to any local bars in Beijing. I told him that even I didn't go to those places, much less take a foreigner there. To me, side-street bars were places for noisy young factory workers and retired manual laborers. I had never seen a woman in a Beijing bar.

"So it is beneath your dignity to sit among them?" Ron snapped sarcastically. He was not far from the truth.

Here in a campus bar, with muffled lights and soft music in the background, I still felt uncomfortble being out with such a young woman. The next time we went there, Judy brought along another one of her students who joined us for a beer. A few sessions later, Jean asked me if I wanted to try another place. This time we went at noon to a restaurant in Greek-town, north of the campus. The waiter greeted Jean warmly, so I assumed she was a regular customer.

Jean asked me if I wanted to try their gyros. I, of course, was interested in tasting any Greek food under her guidance. The small restaurant was quiet, and I felt at ease talking with her over the platter of gyros and raw onions. The food tasted so good that I would afterward go back to Greektown many times for more gyros.

One day Ron wanted to take me out for a meal and asked me where I wanted to go. I chose Greektown. We went this time to a fancy restaurant called the Greek Islands. I didn't want any of the flaming cheese pie (saganaki) Ron suggested, though it looked attractive, and I didn't enjoy most of the other dishes Ron ordered, including the famous stewed leg of lamb in milk and a plateful of unknown expensive delicacies. Whereas Jean and I could eat inexpensively at the gyros place, Ron paid forty dollars for this meal at the exclusive Greek restaurant. The high price itself dulled my appetite. I later told Ron that he had paid not for the food, but for my gourmet food lesson.

CHAPTER NINE

I TRY FARM LIFE

當試農夫生活

No sooner had I expressed my interest in seeing an American farm than Henry Fulkerson, a friend from the U.S.-China People's Friendship Association, arranged for me to visit the Swisher family in Marshall, Missouri. Fulkerson sent me a bus ticket and details of the trip, describing sights I would see along the way. He told me that this was his way of repaying the people who had been so kind to him when he visited China.

Thus I boarded a cross-country bus at 6 A.M. on August 3, 1981, to go to Kansas City by way of St. Louis. The bus traveled along a highway flanked by corn and bean fields that continued out across the miles. The year 1981 promised a good harvest in the United States, with farm export alone expected to reach $45 billion.

My plan had been to take a nap on the bus, but this was thwarted by an eager young theology student who sat next to me and talked to me about Christ and the Bible. I responded by talking about Buddhism and Confucianism, though not with as much enthusiasm. When my religious friend finally reached his destination, I was left to my own thoughts.

What struck me most during the many hours that followed was the vastness of this land. China has a population five times that of the United States, while the United States has five times the amount of China's arable land. Eighty percent of the Chinese people live in the countryside, struggling to produce enough food to satisfy a billion people. Less than 4 percent of the American people live on farms. All the way from Chicago to Marshall, across the states of Illinois and Missouri, I saw no one actually working in the fields. This was the month of August, the time when one would see Chinese peasants working their hardest in the fields, hoeing corn and weeding rice.

In the heartland of America, farmers have replaced manual labor with machines, crop rotation, fertilizers, herbicides and pesticides. I did see an airplane in the sky spraying bean fields with some kind of pesticide. I also saw isolated farmhouses dozens of miles from one another sitting in the middle of huge lawns. On the northern China plains, one never sees isolated farmhouses; villages of several dozen families are the rule. The Chinese government, of course, encourages peasants to produce as much food as possible on every foot of available land. The U.S. government, on the other hand, pays the American farmer not to grow crops in order to maintain higher market prices. I saw large stretches of land that were left fallow, growing only wild grass. The abundant natural resources give people wealth and spare them a lot of worry. "The United States is God's country," as Americans like to say.

I arrived in Marshall at 9 P.M., greeted warmly by Mr. Swisher as I stepped off the bus. We drove out to the farm which Mr. Swisher told me was incorporated and covered 3,000 acres. The Swishers have a large family, including three adult sons, two adult daughters and a son-in-law. Henry Fulkerson had assured me that they were friendly, but I could not have anticipated how friendly they would be. I was afraid that two weeks would be a long time and that I would become a bore and be bored. But as we talked the first night, I knew that my worries were unfounded. Their friendship was genuine; they were not fussy, not overly polite.

On the first day of my visit, I went with the young people to cut cottonweed in the bean fields. We worked and talked and drank ice water from the same jug. The day was hot, and the scorching heat drained my strength. I had not expected that American farmers still do such strenuous work. I happily quit this work early in the afternoon to go with Marty, the Swisher's elder daughter, to bale hay in the air-conditioned cabin of a tractor. The others continued to work in the fields.

Marty, twenty-seven, had a job teaching at an elementary school in Denver, a thousand miles from home. She came home every summer vacation and helped with the field work. Of medium height and slim stature, she had abundant energy. She climbed up to the rooftop of a storehouse to patch a few cracks. I climbed the same thirty-foot-high ladder against a protruding eave and felt my knees shaking as I reached the top—I dared go no farther.

I liked Marty immediately because of her conscientiousness toward work. I felt she had one of my best qualities—or I had her's—the sense of obligation toward work instead of just toward personal relationships. This quality, I find, often offends people. When the two of us worked with Jean, the younger daughter, Jean would say to me, kiddingly, "You must be careful, she's a slave driver." Later Jean would say, "I am thirsty," and she would leave the fields for twenty minutes to find the water jug. Still later she might say, "I have to go back earlier today," and leave Marty behind to take over her rows of beans.

One day at noon Marty suggested that Jean and I go back to the house for lunch. She wanted to finish the plot. When I returned to the field after lunch, she was still working. At the end of the day I told her the farm needed someone like her to run it. She deflected this statement by talking about inequality in the United States. "The rich have too much, and there are too many poor," she said. "Our country is a rich country. Everyone should be given a due share." She sounded like a socialist.

Jean, twenty-three, had a simple and straightforward attitude toward the farm. "I hate working in the fields," she said. She had quit a day-care job in a small town to come back home after she married a former truck driver, who was now working on the farm. Jean was looking anxiously for another day-care job in Marshall, twenty-five miles east of the farm.

Both Bob and Stan, the younger brothers, were home for summer vacation from the college they attended in Kansas City. "They come back to earn pocket money," Jean told me. Both of them worked diligently and each of them had been able to buy a new car with their "pocket money."

Al, the oldest son and a college graduate, was the only Swisher child working full time on the farm. He was twenty-six, a sinewy yet small man who worked relentlessly and who would complain all the time of being tired. The year before, he had become so tired working on the farm all year that he went off to find a new, easier life in the city. He stayed in San Francisco for three months, sleeping on a floor with several Mexicans. He spent all his money and then came back to the farm.

"I never interfere with their lives," Mr. Swisher told me. "I never ask them where they are going. I pay them well, and only hope I can keep them on the farm." I doubted if he could do so. Malta Bend, a small town seven miles west of the farm, had a population of 342, only three more persons than it had ten years before. Young people were leaving to work in the big cities after they completed college. I couldn't comprehend the point when he explained how he paid his sons and daughters according to rules, treating them like employees. It was hard for me to understand because my own grandfather shared the whole family income among his children.

Figures don't make much sense to me, but before I had come to Missouri, I had done a little reading and had learned that the average farm in Illinois and Missouri was 250 to 300 acres in size. I thought their three thousand acres must be a huge area. It was; Mr. Swisher took a whole afternoon to drive me around on a tour of his farm. His big powerful car bumped along the edge of the fields, pressing down the tall grass. We visited three farmhouses, two of which were empty. They had belonged to former farmers, who had owned smaller farms that were now part of Mr. Swisher's acreage. He said, on hearing me say how remarkable it would be to live in such beautiful and quiet houses, "I'll give one of them to you and your family, if you want to stay." He was not joking. I almost wished it were possible.

During that four-hour tour of his farm, Mr. Swisher often got out of the car and went into the bean fields to spray herbicides on the tall grass. The sun was hot and the air in the fields was close. We waded among bean stalks that came up to my shoulders in height. Very soon I found it difficult to breathe, but Mr. Swisher pressed on with big strides to deeper spots where clusters of Johnson grass stood above the beans.

In one bean plot I saw a brand new, bright red tractor. Mr. Swisher told me it cost 50 thousand dollars. I was amazed at the fact that such an expensive tractor was left in the open fields at the mercy of the elements. I also saw water trailers and tractors of several kinds standing around in the dirt, as if they had been there all year. The machinery needed at least a dozen maintenance workers to keep it in good shape, but Mr. Swisher could afford to hire only one.

Al told me the next day when we were working on a broken conveyor system, "It is more costly to hire people to maintain the equipment than to buy new machines." The motor was rusted from having been left in the open too long. That day, Al drove to Marshall three times to buy parts for the conveyor.

Another day I tried my hand at operating three different tractors. Al, ignoring my statement that I didn't know how to drive, had asked me to bring over a truck. I got in, started it up and drove away with Jean beside me. I could only hope that between God and Confucius, all would not be lost. On still another day, I mowed the grass on their two-acre front yard with a small tractor. It took me three hours to cut it all. I later told Mr. Swisher that his front yard was so large it would support a Chinese peasant family of four.

Marty wanted to introduce me to country and western music, and so we went bar-hopping on Saturday night. She and her friend tried to persuade me to dance, but I was too shy to try. A young farmer, somewhat drunk, offered to buy each of us a beer, and I watched two farmers bet $15 on a game of pool. Another night, Jean and her husband treated me to beer and barbecued chicken. In the court-yard of their home, one of the three Mr. Swisher had shown me on the tour, was a huge apple tree. Wind had knocked part of it down, and lovely big apples lay on the ground rotting. This was not intentional waste; instead, it is what happens in a situation where there is so much abundance that a few dozen extra apples are not needed. While I stayed in their home, Mrs. Swisher served great quantities of food of high quality. The family ate much better than most of my city friends. I had shrimp nearly every lunch—farmers have their big meal at noon.

The word "dating" took on more meaning for me while I was visiting the Swishers. In China, if a single man takes a single woman out for dinner or to a park, it of course means they are "talking love." And if a young man has more than one girlfriend he is considered a philanderer. Worse is said about any girl who goes out with more than one man. Yet in the two weeks that I stayed on that Missouri farm,

Stan brought home three different girlfriends at different times. "He has so many girls," Jean told me, "that he changes to a different one every day." I wondered how these girls must have regarded themselves, going out with a young man when they knew he had other girlfriends.

Mr. Swisher was proud that there was a Chinese restaurant in Marshall. Twice the family took me there; the restaurant was full both times.

"I'm from Chicago," the Chinese restaurateur told me. He was glad to meet a fellow countryman in such a remote place. "Business in Chicago was so bad that when I heard someone was selling a restaurant in Marshall, I bought it and moved here, hoping I would have better luck—I did. Ours is the only Chinese restaurant in town. People used to drive seventy-five miles west to Kansas City or east to Columbia for a Chinese dinner. Now they eat here. The local paper offered me free advertising at our opening. I said no because I was afraid I'd be flooded with customers. I didn't even put out a sign the first day. People came early and waited in line. Every night I have a hundred cutomers, but I only have one cook, so I have to help in the kitchen." Although he was complaining about so many customers, I knew he was quite satisfied. He hurried back to the kitchen when an American waitress told him the cook needed help.

The cook later took a break to come out and talk to me. He didn't speak any English. "I work from morning till night, fifteen hours a day, six days a week. Out of twenty-four hours I stand two-thirds of the time." He was genuinely complaining.

"Where is your famiy?" I asked.

"They are in Kansas. They don't want to come out here. There are no other Chinese in Marshall."

He wanted very much to talk to me, since I was the first Chinese besides his boss that he had been able to talk to in a long time. But he was called back to the kitchen when two new customers appeared. The owner came out with free desert to show his affection to a countryman. "I pay the cook $1,000 a month plus free room and board," he told me.

"Why don't you hire another cook?" I asked.

"I can't afford it right now, but I will, certainly I will."

I knew that $1,000 a month was a big sum for this employer. The Swishers asked me about the food. "It's excellent," I said, after a moment's hesitation, not wanting to ruin my countrymen's reputation.

I went to the kitchen to say goodbye to the boss and the cook. "Please excuse our poor skill," the owner said. "You know we don't have time or enough hands to prepare carefully." What could I say? Could I tell the Swishers the dishes could not really be called fine food by Chinese standards? These men were, after all, my countrymen. In my heart I hoped the restaurateur wouldn't become too greedy; otherwise, he would have to find an even more remote town in which to open a new Chinese restaurant. But I wondered if he would be able to find a Chinese cook to go with him, even for $1,000 a month and free room and board.

One evening, after an early supper, Al drove me to see the Missouri River, which joins the Mississippi. I had read Mark Twain's *Life on the Mississippi* and had been fascinated by the scenes he described. Originally I had intended to stay in St. Louis for a day or two on my way here, in order to see the Mississippi, but I had nowhere to stay, and the blackish water and dirty surroundings I saw from the bus as we entered St. Louis dulled my interest. Now in this part of Missouri it was easy to visualize Mark Twain's life a hundred years earlier, with its wide flat land, wild woods, and turbulent waters, still seemingly untouched by humans. Twain's landing places for steamboats are missing, but a railroad runs along the side of the river, passing grain bins at desolate stations.

On my first Sunday morning at the farm, I went to church with Mr. Swisher. I was moved when he solemnly thanked God for having a Chinese visitor in their home. At

106

the Sunday family dinner, Mr. Swisher's ninety-one-year-old mother, his brother and wife, and two of his sons' girlfriends were guests at the table set in my honor. The grandmother said a prayer before the meal, once again thanking God for my visit to her family. It was tempting, even for one as strongly influenced by atheism as I have been, to join in the calm and good feelings brought about by the family's religious practices.

My visit to Marshall gave me a chance to meet people in the community. I was invited to speak to a breakfast meeting of the Optimists Club, a local businessmen's and farmers' organization. I liked the club's name; I hoped people all over the world would be as optimistic about the future of the world as these people seemed to be. At the meeting Mr. Swisher said that everyone throughout the world should have the same language so that people could understand each other better. He also said I was their first visitor from the People's Republic of China, and that my stay made it possible for them to know more about China. I told the club about my work in Beijing and about the life of Chinese peasants. They asked a lot of questions: Is every Chinese a Communist? Are there rich people and poor people in China? Does China have a welfare system like the one in the United States? How do the aged people live in China?

I told the club members that there are no television stars, football players or plastic surgeons who are paid tens of thousands of dollars in China, as there are in the U.S.; and that a Chinese minister of state makes about two hundred dollars a month, only three times more than a skilled factory worker. I said that our people are not starving; we "ration" what food we have, which is not much. Perhaps this is why China does not have many overweight people. I said that diet pills were strange to me. In China I had never heard the term "on a diet." I also told them that Chinese people are a hardworking people. If we had as much rich and arable land as there is in the U.S., the Chinese people would probably produce more than American farmers do. I concluded that at first I thought the United States was so rich because it had such advanced technology and science. But now that I had come to Marshall and seen the rich land, I thought that the prosperity came from the earth. The surplus wealth from the land supported the manpower needed to develop science and technology. The audience seemed to appreciate my talk. They thanked me and invited me to return to Marshall again in the future to tell them more about life in China.

I had only one disturbing experience during my visit with the Swishers, as Al and I were driving home from the Missouri River. We saw a group of people walking in the dark along the highway. I asked Al if they needed a ride and he turned the pickup truck around. The group, who were desperately hoping someone would give them a lift, turned out to be a family of three adults and three children—two young girls under thirteen and a boy around seven. They asked us to drive them to a crossroad where they might be able to hitch a ride. They had hitchhiked all the way to Missouri from South Carolina, looking for odd jobs on farms. They had by now spent all their savings.

Al and I each gave them ten dollars, hoping they would have a hot meal and a roof over them that night, then dropped them off at the crossroad. The older girl, about twelve, waved to us in gratitude. My heart ached seeing this lovely girl, dog-tired and face smeared with dirt. I asked Al why he couldn't have given them work, since the Swisher farm needed a lot of farm hands. "It's too expensive to hire people," Al said thoughtfully. Why, I asked myself, can't the country deal with its migrant worker problem? The United States is such a rich country that I wondered why there are still people as poor as this.

Before I realized it, the two weeks had passed. I felt sad at the thought of leaving this quiet place, with its fields, woods in a wild state, great expanses of land, and especially the people to whom I had become so close. I had planned to leave on Monday, but from early Sunday morning on, I felt restless; by afternoon I could stand it no longer. I wanted to get the departure over with, and so I left that night.

Seeing me off, Mrs. Swisher said, "You have become one of the family. You are welcome to join this family anytime you wish." Mr. Swisher said he would send me a bus ticket whenever I wished to come back to the farm. After arriving in the United States in December 1980, I found that being homesick was my greatest torture, but I didn't feel this while I was staying with them. For this reason, I will always have the greatest respect for those kind people in Marshall, Missouri.

CHAPTER TEN

TELEPHONES, TVS, AND COMMUNES

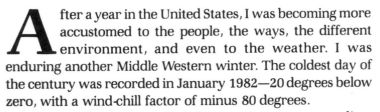

After a year in the United States, I was becoming more accustomed to the people, the ways, the different environment, and even to the weather. I was enduring another Middle Western winter. The coldest day of the century was recorded in January 1982—20 degrees below zero, with a wind-chill factor of minus 80 degrees.

In the middle of the cold spell, Meg Moritz, a news editor at Chicago's Channel 5 television station, had planned a Sunday evening party. I called her in the morning to check whether or not the party was still on. She said yes, but told me that some of her friends couldn't get their cars started in the cold and wouldn't be coming, but she would be glad if I would still come and bring a friend. "There is a lot of food," she assured me.

I called Ronit Loewenstern, a journalism student, to see if she would like to go. She said she would, and could bring a friend. I was glad I had found a chance to see Ronit, or "Ron" as we called her. In her early twenties, Ron was spirited and aggressive and quite attractive in her own way. I had met Ron during a Thanksgiving trip sponsored by the

International House at the University of Chicago. The trip to Danville—150 miles south of Chicago—was designed to give sixty foreign students a chance to visit a small Illinois city outside the large metropolis.

Ron had attracted my attention because of what I read on the tag attached to her bag: "*The Star*—South Africa—Associate Editor." South Africa is always described in China as a reactionary country of racial oppression. My impression of it was of separated white, black and colored communities, of whites exploiting and brutally killing natives who toiled on the plantations.

I approached her and introduced myself. "We are colleagues," I said. "I would like to talk to you."

"Sure, glad to." She sounded quite casual and self-assured, and she was willing to tell me the situation in her country.

I had never realized there were any whites in South Africa fighting for the interests of the blacks. But here was a white woman, born of British parents, a liberal descendant of the British who opposed the government's apartheid policy. Ron told how they stood up against the conservative descendants of the Dutch for the rights of blacks. We agreed to talk again after we returned to Chicago. So, "Borrowing flowers to present to the Buddha," as we say in Chinese, I used Meg's party as an excuse to see my new friend.

It was dusk already at four o'clock when I set off into a blizzard. The moment I stepped out of the door, my face became numb. The wind was blowing savagely, whipping up snow dust on the rooftops. I ran the two blocks from my house to the Western train station, not passing a soul on the street. I was shivering when I reached the shelter inside the closed ticket office, which was as dead as a ghost town. (On Sundays they sold tickets on the train.) The swinging doors had blown open, and the draft was painfully cold. I pulled my down jacket tightly around me, regretting that I hadn't put on my woolen underwear. I waited there because on the platform downstairs I would be unprotected from the wind. I felt the curious looks behind the windows of cars speeding by on Western, and could imagine the people inside saying, "Look at that poor Chinese fellow. what the hell is he doing out in this weather!"

Finally, I could no longer stand the curious looks of the people in the passing cars, and I walked down to the platform and into the wind, pulling down the hat I had bought at a discount store so that it would partially hide my face. A line from one of Lu Xun's famous poems came to mind: "Hiding my face as I was passing a shopping street..." I had lost the warm woolen hat my wife had knitted for me.

After an unbearably long time the train came. I felt relieved to see that the train was half-filled with passengers, and that I was not the only one entirely dependent on public transportation in such bad weather. I looked at my watch; in fact, I had been in the station for only ten minutes.

As it grew dark, I rode the train all the way to the north terminal on the Evanston line. I walked to Meg's house in the middle of a seeming wilderness. Only a few lonely houses stood blurred by the snow flurries among the trees. Why, I wondered, do people choose such a place to live?

It was pleasant and warm inside the house. Meg was single, as were Barbara, Judy and several other career women I knew. And each of them had a good income and a nice house—big enough for three Beijing families to live in.

I was the first guest to arrive, and after using several tissues on my dripping nose and drinking two cups of warm Japanese rice wine by the fireplace, I felt my blood begin to circulate again. Meg introduced me to her house guest, a Philippine woman from Hawaii. Five minutes later Ron arrived, stamping her feet on the mat at the door.

"Hi, Liu, warm my hands," she called in her ringing British accent, stretching out her icy hands to me. I rubbed them in mine as I introduced her to Meg. I was surprised later I had not felt embarrassed by my action. It came so naturally this time. My two roommates told me I had changed. Perhaps I had, not only did I now hold their hands, I even hugged a couple of women I knew well. I was becoming westernized.

I looked into Ron's merry eyes. "How did you get here?" "Walking." She laughed. "No, I am kidding. John wanted to walk. I insisted on the train. Oh, this is John." She motioned to the man who had come through the door with her.

John was a handsome young New Zealander in his mid-twenties. He was going to journalism school, too. In contrast with the energetic Ron, her friend was quite reserved and quiet-spoken, and I liked his manner. Shortly afterwards, Rohsenow, a professor at Circle, arrived with a young woman from Taiwan. Meg announced that the five of us were the bravest people in the world for defying the storm and coming to her untimely party.

It is said that the United States is a melting pot. I could not help being struck by the nationalities of these seven people: two Americans, the hostess and the professor; two Chinese representing the antagonists, Mainland China and Taiwan; a South African Caucasian; a Filipino; and a New Zealander. I don't know whether Meg intentionally invited this mixed group, but I doubt it. Around her comfortable fireplace seven ordinary people sat together—color, features and accents as forgotten as the storm outside. While we talked, jumping from one country to another, I wondered if the United Nations ever threw small parties like this.

As the evening drew toward its end, Ron said she was going to give a party during the coming spring break. "I will invite one person from each country to my party, and ask each one to bring something that particularly represents their country. Will that be fun?"

"Certainly," I agreed with enthusiasm. "Am I on your guest list?"

"Of course. You are my first guest."

I suggested that Ron name her party the International

Club. I recalled what I had told the reporter from the Danville paper at Thanksgiving time. I thanked the Danville residents for their kindness in providing an opportunity to bring people from a dozen countries together. Such a project, I said, should be carried out on a worldwide scale. When ordinary people come together, and understand each other, they make a lot more sense than politicians. People need this kind of person-to-person contact, and it's possible that it might even prevent wars.

The logs in the fireplace sparked and roared for a moment. The faces glowed in the reflection of the flames and candlelight. We all remained oblivious to the freezing weather, reluctant to leave. And then it was time to leave, time to go our separate ways. Professor Rohsenow drove me home that night so I was spared walking once more through the now even more frigid Midwestern night.

• • •

My original dread of using the telephone was completely gone; in fact, I became particularly attached to this handy convenience. One month after I arrived in the United States, I called Fengyun in Beijing, calculating the time carefully to make sure that she was in her office; otherwise she would have to call me back from our neighborhood phone. She was excited and cried. The phone was new to me and I didn't even know how to carry on a long-distance conversation since this was my first. It was difficult then for me to make the call, yet it was very good to hear Fengyun's voice.

Although the telephone has been in existence for more than a century, it is still a rarity for most Chinese. Even in highly professional units, such as the offices of my own magazine, there are only a few direct-dial phones. And only three of the two hundred staff members of *China Reconstructs* have telephones in their homes. It was not until 1980 that Ione Kramer, an American woman who had worked for the magazine for more than twenty years, had a home phone installed, and she received this only because

114

she was a foreign expert working in China. It would be nice to have a telephone at home, but since no other friends or relatives of mine are privileged to have their own phone, I seldom telephone anyone in Beijing and don't really feel inconvenienced. From central Beijing where we live, I once rode my bicycle for forty minutes to a northeast suburb just to tell my father-in-law that my wife was not feeling well and we could not come to his home for dinner.

In recent years, the Beijing city government has installed a great number of public phones in the neighborhoods, averaging one per thousand households. They have been installed either in private homes, where there is someone home all the time to take calls, or in stores or service centers. Our neighborhood phone is in the milk distribution center, where the woman who takes care of the milk bottles also manages the two telephones. When the telephone rings for any resident in my area, she records the caller's number and hangs up. Then she sends one of her grandchildren or her retired husband to find the resident in one of seven high-rise apartment buildings that compose my neighborhood. From below they shout out the name of the recipient to all the apartment dwellers in the 14 floors above. If the recipient is home and hears the shouts, he or she runs down the stairway to the street below (the elevator operator works only certain hours) and then to the telephone at the milk distribution center. The fee for all of this is seven cents—three for the messenger and four for the call back.

• • •

By the time I had been in Chicago for five months, I calculated that I had logged 750 hours of TV time. Before I left China an American language expert told me that the best way to understand American life was to watch TV. "Six hours a day," he told me. So I started watching the first night I arrived in the United States, in the embassy's dining hall. Almost every day after that, I sat before a television set for six hours, the length of time my family watched it in a week in China.

As a journalist trying to learn both the English language and about American culture, television proved to be the most valuable source. All this watching, of course, was from the point of view of a journalist who is forty years old, a man at the age at which Confucius says one is supposed to know the world well and not be easily affected by outside influences. If my twelve-year-old son had come to the United States, I would surely have warned him, "Watch out when you watch TV!"—I say "watch out" because some shows undoubtedly have a bad influence on young minds. People on the screen are shown driving cars wildly, brawling in the streets, shooting at each other, killing one another, being stripped of their clothes and raped.

I was shocked when I heard on the television evening news a report of three girls in their teens shooting a man to death on Chicago's north side. The girls did it deliberately, as if they were playing a part in a thrilling TV film. But, unfortunately, so many deaths are reported on television that many people eventually become indifferent to the news of murders reported between the Dow Jones stock averages and the weather report.

I don't want to imply that all television shows are bad, or that most crime stems from TV. As a matter of fact, I liked the greater part of what I saw. I liked the news programs on all channels; Walter Jacobsen's "Perspective" and Ted Koppell's "ABC Nightline" were my favorites. I also liked Johnny Carson's jokes, and the "Wild, Wild World of Animals" on public television never failed to arouse my admiration for the people who take such marvelous pictures. From "Nova" I acquired as much knowledge in a few hours as I might by reading volumes of books. And when I was watching "You Asked for It," I usually wondered how much money they had to spend sending their reporters all over the world.

In using television as my English class instead of as entertainment, I didn't care whether the programs were old or new, or what the contents might be—even the commercials proved of help, since they were repeated hundreds of times. This aided my pronunciation just as the tape recorder did when I played again and again the phrases that had been taped at the Speech and Hearing Clinic. Through TV commercials I also came to know many things that I would otherwise never have learned. For example, it would have been embarrassing to ask a salesman what those egg-shaped objects on the store shelf were. The TV commercials clearly said they were L'eggs—"pantyhose as smooth as silk." On the screen, the high-stepping dance of a pretty girl showed that this pantythose would come to the top of a woman's thighs.

Almost every half hour a dog-food commercial would come on. A voice would say, "Come and get it," and then the dogs on the screen would begin barking, running and jumping, while the off-stage voice enumerated the virtues of the dog food. Next, there would be a commercial for diet pills. It was a matter of curiosity to me why the women in the diet commercials were always very slender *before* taking the pills. I was also curious as to why Americans encourage dogs to eat more and humans to eat less.

In the United States food is so plentiful that much is wasted and many people are afraid of eating too much and becoming fat. However, I did read in newspapers of an old woman eating dog food because she could afford nothing else, of poor families in Chicago running out of food stamps and starving, and of several persons dying of the cold in the winter of 1981-82.

In China, food has been a major concern of everyone's daily life for a thousand years. We have had to struggle to produce enough to eat. The amount of food per person is regulated since we want to guarantee that all will have some and no one will starve. In late September 1968, the most disturbing year of the Cultural Revolution, I went with two dozen office workers to a mountain village thirty miles north of Beijing to help with the harvest. The peasants there had had to tide themselves over on unripened potatoes until the autumn harvest.

• • •

Every time there was a school vacation I was faced with the problem of finding something to do. Long before final exams, I would begin hoping someone might suggest some activity that would enable me to be with Americans and to learn more about life in the U.S.

During the 1982 spring vacation I had two choices. The first was to go to the Missouri farm again. My farmer friend had called twice asking me to come. The other choice was to go to Madison, Wisconsin, to visit Karen, a laboratory worker at the University of Wisconsin. Karen had gotten my address from the *Reader*, a Chicago newspaper that published a story on my life in the United States. She had written several times urging me to spend a long weekend with her and her boyfriend.

In spite of all the temptations of being able to drive a tractor again, the thought of a twelve-hour bus trip to the Missouri farm took the edge off my interest. So I decided to take the shorter trip to Madison. I set off at noon, March 19th, in a chilly rain.

The bus trip was far from pleasant, as the rain turned to sleet, then snow, and then rain again, blurring my view of the countryside. I sat there wishing I could meet somebody like the young theology student I had talked to on the bus to Missouri the previous summer. This time, the seat next to me was empty. A girl sat by herself on the seat in front of me. Several times I was tempted to talk to her, but my narrow sense of propriety bolted me to my seat. I was left to fantasize about how I might conduct the conversation if I dared to lean forward.

Madison is a much cleaner and quieter city than Chicago.

I imagined how very charming it would be when the lakes thawed and the trees began to turn green, but I was here two weeks too soon. Karen met me at the bus station and drove me to her home, stopping first at a bean curd shop. I was amused to see American women working in the shop making bean products Chinese-style. We bought two bottles of soy milk and two pieces of bean curd. I decided I would tell my friends in Chicago about this place; some of them might be interested in setting up such a shop. The business would no doubt be good, since Chicago has many more oriental residents than Madison does.

Karen had written explaining that she was divorced and living with a boyfriend, and she assured me I would be in a nice family atmosphere. By now I had become used to the U.S. practice of couples living together, so I really didn't need any explanation, but it did surprise me somewhat to find, when I got to her house, that her boyfriend was so young; she was thirty-eight and Paul was only twenty-five. They lived in the western suburbs of Madison, in the middle of hayfields. I can't drive, and there was no public transportation nearby, so all day Saturday, Paul and I had nothing better to do but talk about his plan to renovate the house. Karen had left to attend a religious meeting some fifty miles away. The night before, as we were driving to her home, she had explained a little about her religion, a combination of Christianity and several other religions, including Buddhism. Her beliefs surprised me, but then I think that I will never stop being surprised at some of the strange beliefs I found among Americans.

Back in August 1981, Ron Dorfman got an assignment from a Chicago newspaper to write an article on a community calling itself the Stelle Group, and he asked me if I would like to go with him on the interview. We drove sixty-five miles south of Chicago to a tranquil community of three dozen houses amid cornfields. Malcolm Carnahan, Stelle's elected president, briefed us on their developing program: they had 240 acres of land, a plastics workshop, an experimental ethanol plant, school, and day-care center. Their philosophy of brotherhood was formulated in a little book entitled *The Ultimate Frontier*. They believed in God, but not in Christianity. The doctrine embraced all human races. According to their theory, between 630 B.C. and 550 B.C., five High Adepts were incarnated to spread the truths that would elevate men and prepare them for the coming of Christ. The five were Lao Tze, Buddha, Mahavira, Zoroaster, and Confucius. I felt honored by the fact that two Chinese, Lao Tze and Confucius, were accepted by this group as harbingers of the enlightened world. The twelve virtues they practiced were devotion, sincerity, tolerance, kindness, patience, precision, efficiency, forbearance, discernment, courage, charity, and humility. I was reminded of the twelve fundamental principles practiced by the Buddhist sect in China.

They gave us a tour of their energy-saving houses—houses built to trap solar heat and to circulate the air so that the structures were warm in winter and cool in summer. In one of their greenhouses, a middle-aged woman was tending tomatoes, squash and other vegetables. She said their goal was self-sufficiency in everything. The surroundings were quiet, not only because Stelle is far away from other human dwellings and traffic thoroughfares, but mainly because members didn't own many cars. Compared with most Chicagoans I had met, the people in this community had few material things.

I asked Ron if he thought it were possible for the Stelle Group to develop their goal of twenty thousand strong by the year 2000. "No," Ron said, "the outside world is too tempting for many to stay here."

I was doubtful, too. The members that I talked to were all college-educated and white. My impression was that they were too idealistic, though they denied they were utopian. "Scholars talk about revolt," one Chinese saying puts it, "but they will never succeed."

Karen had fasted on the morning before her meeting. Paul and I ate barley porridge and toast. The two of them were strict vegetarians—no beef, fish, fowl, eggs or dairy products. When we first sat down at the table, I waited to see if they would say grace. I learned early that it was necessary to do this when eating with an American family. If the family did say grace, I sat quietly until their prayer ended. Karen and Paul put their hands together above the table, their mouths moving quietly. I waited quietly. Later Paul explained that they were not saying a prayer, but were meditating, because Karen believed meditation was good for the health.

The next morning the three of us went to a forest preserve, where I felt the elation I always do in such natural places. A deer ran by, spring water gurgled, and an old Indian burial ground we walked through evoked in me a feeling of wonder. After the woods, we went in to see downtown Madison and to visit the capitol.

Karen, in her letter, had told me to bring swimming trunks for the sauna. I didn't check my dictionary and thought she meant we would swim in the lakes pictured on the postcards she sent me. I had swum in the frozen lakes of Beijing and looked forward to doing the same in the United States. A sauna, I soon learned, is a steam bath. That afternoon Karen took me into a small room of the house where the temperature was above 150 degrees. Within three minutes I was sweating profusely. Karen had wrapped herself in a towel, but as the heat went up and she sweated more and more, the towel slipped to her waist. I kept my eyes from looking in her direction. I had already learned that American women are not as inhibited as Chinese women, and I had read about a hundred Los Angeles women parading topless to demand equality with men in dress codes. I had also read about Chicago's nude nightclubs. But I didn't like that kind of exposure.

Karen wanted to give me a massage to clear my sinuses, another interesting experience for me. She was one of many Americans who are taking up Chinese acupuncture and massage. I felt her soothing fingers as well as the bare breasts that were hanging over my head. Sitting in a small space with a half-naked female friend definitely made me nervous. I wondered if I would ever get over my Chinese sense of morality.

I spent the next morning with Paul in their vegetable garden, where he and Karen both liked to work. "I like to take time off to work in my garden, so I only work four days a week," Paul told me. "I make enough money to carry on. Why do people need so much?

In the afternoon I left these two nice people and took the bus back to Chicago. I was just in time to catch a good dinner at my house, where my roommates were entertaining four Taiwan friends. After three days in Madison on vegetables and cereal, I was starving; I stuffed my stomach with meat and fish.

CHAPTER ELEVEN

AMERICAN STANDARDS

The *New York Times* correspondent in Beijing wrote in an article how he was amused to see a Chinese girl in Shanghai wearing blue jeans (they are called cowboy pants in China). I also remember that twenty years ago the *Beijing Daily* reported that, as a sign of social degeneration in Yugoslavia, young people bought smuggled blue jeans at one hundred dollars a pair. In the United States, almost everyone seemed to be wearing them. I came to love the pair Ron gave me at Christmas; they were durable, casual, and in them I felt conscious of how well they fit my figure.

But now I had heard in a letter from Fengyun that some young people in Beijing had started wearing their hair long, sporting colorful and fancily cut clothes and short skirts. Not only that, they were kissing in the streets and public parks. "It is disgusting, Fengyun said, "to see them in western suits, swaggering along the streets, just like circus monkeys in costume." She was appalled to see my youngest brother and his girlfriend touch their foreheads together at the holiday family dinner table. "They paid no heed at all to the presence of my father, brother, sisters-in-law, and young niece and nephew," she said bitterly. "All this they learned from western culture. They are imitating U.S. magazines and films."

Fengyun is one of the million educated Chinese who have access to western culture, compared to the 999 million who have no chance for this sophistication. She works for a government publishing department dealing with foreign countries. And she is still young at thirty-five. Nevertheless, here she was complaining about the western life-style entering China along with the advanced western technology. Things had definitely changed since I left in November 1980, and they would change much more by 1982 when I would return. I would need less time to adjust to my former Chinese life than if I had returned to China even one year earlier.

But how much could the West change China? With a history of three thousand years, Chinese traditions are deeply rooted and foreign influence does not penetrate easily. Throughout Chinese history outsiders have tried to impose their culture, but the outcome has always been the same: the outsiders became Chinese. The Mongolians and Manchus, who ruled China for hundreds of years at different times, finally lost their identity.

Confucius taught that obedience is the fundamental virtue that guarantees a unified country and a harmonious family life. Harmony means social conformity and integration. And though academic and artistic contributions are encouraged, aggressiveness in dress or manner is scorned. An example of this conformity is the great achievement rendered by Dr. Sun Yat Sen—pioneer of the modern Chinese revolution that overthrew the Qing Dynasty in 1911—when he designed the Sun Yat-sen jacket. It had a tight collar, much like the British army uniform of that time, and unlike the western-style open lapelled coat. The new style soon replaced the old jackets, which were clumsy and used more material. The Chinese Communists made slight modifications and adopted this jacket as their cadre uniform. In the West it became known as the Mao jacket, and has been one of the national symbols of China for the past thirty years.

The concept of this jacket conforms with the Chinese teaching of modesty, taught very early to children. They are told not to differ from others in appearance, not to be conspicuous, or they will provoke gossip. "She is frivolous," people might say if a woman did her hair in a fancy way; or, if she wore western clothing, they might comment, "Her blouse is too open at the neck!"

Of course, this is not the way Americans judge each other. Everyone tries to be different—and sometimes this goes to an extreme. One morning I glanced out of a classroom window to see a bright-colored figure walking across the lawn in front of University Hall. The sun glistened on her scarlet dress and bright red boots; her huge gold earrings sparkled, yet the part that caught the sunshine most was her hair. It was dyed half-red and half-yellow. In China, even a crazy woman would not dare walk out in the open looking like that.

In America, the overriding need to be recognized as an individual is so often expressed in the way one dresses. The exceptions are the teenagers who choose to dress alike and happily submit to the styles dictated by their peers. Parents and schools may not approve of certain fads in clothing yet they find it virtually impossible to control the dress codes. Other than the teenagers, I discovered no restrictions on how people should dress. I never saw two persons dressed identically, except by choice; the businessmen and bank workers on LaSalle Street dressed in three-piece suits and ties, all wearing their wing-tipped shoes. Still, they had enough variety in their outfits to appear different from one another. A young professor at Circle wore a different tie and shirt every day, even if he wore the same suit. With all the clothing changes they made every day, there was little chance that two professors would show up looking alike.

Before I went to the United States, I had expected to see hippies and miniskirts on every street. I was told that the average coverage of a woman's body is only 5 percent. I found, of course, that this isn't true, but American women do display the contour of their breasts and hips with deliberate pride, though not as I had expected. In Chicago, many women still wore old-fashioned swimming suits that covered their abdomens. I did see, so often that it no longer surprised me, boys with long hair and beards, immodestly kissing and hugging their girls in public. In Beijing, if I saw a college age boy and girl clinging to each other in an alley, I would pick up my pace, pretending not to see them.

I bought few clothes in the United States, not wanting to spend two hundred dollars for a suit I would never wear back in China. Most of my western Chicago clothes would go into a storage trunk, as my father's had—mere reminders of his ten-year period of service abroad. I wore the same jacket and two pairs of pants all through the seasons, just as I had in Beijing. I thought little of this until two Chinese colleagues from Illinois State University told me they felt embarrassed when they wore the same clothes two days in a row. "Everyone in America changes every day," they said. "We don't have many clothes but we don't want to look shabby. We learned a trick—don't laugh at us. We take off the clothes we wear today and hang them in the closet. Tomorrow we put on another set. The day after tomorrow, we will wear the first set again; then next day, we mix the two sets up and we thus have a new set of clothes."

I laughed, not at my two colleagues, but at people who spend time worrying about what clothes they should wear. It is a waste of time for people to fuss over clothes, and it is also a waste for Chinese to try to find ways to restrict others manner of dress. I hope that Chinese society will become more open, as America is, about the matter of clothing. A few western suits and blue jeans can hardly change centuries of Chinese teaching—history has already proved that. A billion people are like an immense ocean which can easily accomodate a few drops of foreign pigment without changing color. Western life is very appealing to many young Chinese today, who think that a better life can be achieved by adopting western life-styles. Let them try—they will soon learn.

• • •

In January 1982, I was asked to be one of several participants on a night talk-show about China on Chicago's WGN radio station. A woman caller wanted to know if China has freedom. "Freedom," she said, "is the best thing we have in the United States." I didn't really want to discuss such a broad subject in such a limited time. But Rosenburger, the host, pleaded with me with his eyes, and since the other two Chinese participants remained silent, I had to say something. "The Chinese cultural background is entirely different from that of Americans," I said. We have very strong traditions: some are good and some are not so good. We have to find our own way to change, to improve our society. We can't transplant your way of life to China. It just wouldn't work to plunk down the American type of freedom in the middle of China." Out of the Chinese tradition of being polite in a host's house, I didn't mention the abridgments of freedom in recent American history that everyone knows about—the persecutions in the McCarthy period of the 1950s, or the laws that for too long restricted the rights of American minorities.

I thought of a young Chinese sculptor who complained that he didn't have the freedom to develop his abstract art. He blamed the government for this; however, it was never a matter of whether or not the government would grant him permission to create, but rather a question of whether or not the public would accept his work when he completed it. Michelangelo, because he was born in Italy, was able to become famous by creating statues of nudes. Gu Hongzhong, who lived at about the same time but was born in China, was able to become famous by painting fully dressed, beautiful women. Different cultures simply develop along different lines, with varying modes of acceptability. For example, the base of my desk lamp in Chicago was in the form of a kneeling nude woman. I would never dare to display this in my office in China, not because of the authorities, but because I would be afraid of the gossip among my colleagues.

Americans really understand little about Chinese society and tradition and they readily pass judgment on China according to their own history and culture, and their prejudice against communism. An irony is that the more one learns about China, the more bewildered and confused he will become until, over time, he may finally be able to sort out the complexities. There is truth in the saying that if an American has stayed in China for several months he could write a book about her; if he has stayed for more than a year he could write a long article; and if he has stayed more than that he could write nothing. This was the case with some of the Americans I have worked with in my Beijing office. One American I knew in Beijing, who returned to the United States after staying in China for a year, wrote an article full of negative impressions and hostile remarks for a Chicago magazine. In our many arguments about China before he left, I told him that the dozen Chinese he associated with in Beijing were not the "real" Chinese, that these people did not represent the whole nation. I could not convince him that he had not truly come to an understanding of China—almost as if he knew China better than I, regardless of my broad knowledge of Chinese history and tradition.

• • •

In general, Americans practice much more freedom in sex matters and in chosing the kinds of relationships they will have. Of course, things are changing in China, too. Ten years ago, it would have been unthinkable for Chinese college students to have sexual relations outside of marriage; but now they do, covertly. In American schools, it is not uncommon for a casual date to end up in bed, and few would even notice. A Chinese woman student I knew shared an apartment with an American student. The Chinese soon moved out to live with two other Chinese students because the American woman's boyfriend often stayed overnight in their apartment.

Two American-educated Chinese translators at the Foreign Languages Press were divorced after thirty years of marriage, but they continued to work in offices next to each other and to go to one another's offices to chat and joke. It was as if they had never had such a relationship as marriage. "They have drunk foreign ink," their colleagues commented, "so, they are open-minded in such matters." To me, marriage is a life-long commitment. How could these people regard it so lightly?

In 1980 China passed a revised marriage law that makes the divorce procedure simpler and easier; still, the divorce rate is very low. The general public doesn't have a very high regard for divorced people. Friends and relatives will do everything possible to prevent a separation if the relationship between a couple sours. Furthermore, relatives and friends feel it their duty to find a mate for any unmarried person who is over thirty. A single person of that age may even be teased for being "too dumb to find a wife or husband."

After being in Chicago for more than a year, I had at least three dozen American friends and acquaintances, primarily middle-class people with good educations and incomes. I didn't see among them the kind of loose sexual life that I continually saw on TV; yet what bewildered me was the fact that among those thirty or more people there were only three married couples. The others either lived alone or simply "lived together"—a phenomenon unheard of in China.

I was puzzled when David, a newspaper journalist, introduced the young woman in his home to me as his "girlfriend" instead of as his "wife." It took me quite a while to find out that it has become acceptable in the United States for a man and woman to live together without marriage. "You pay less income tax by reporting as single," a man involved in such a relationship told me, but I found his explanation too glib.

With all the living space available, Americans may choose exactly how they want to live. My friend Ron lives alone. He, and many others like him, could have had nice families and raised healthy children, but they preferred the single life. Whenever I went to Ron's home, or to the homes of other single friends, I found their nicely furnished apartments desolate and empty—I even found it difficult to call their homes "homes." A home should be composed of husband and wife; to complete it, there should be children.

My less affluent single friends rented apartments together and split the cost two or three ways; none of them were gays or lesbians. I often wondered where they could seek comfort when they were ill or depressed. The family is like a cell, a basic structure of life. These people were like many drifting molecules without a nucleus to bind them together. Free, indeed!

One day I was introduced to an attractive woman in her early thirties who had been divorced a year earlier. She had a two-bedroom apartment, as neat and exquisite as the person herself. As a construction worker, she had to go to work during the day and leave two lovely daughters, ages seven and five, behind. I asked her who was taking care of them while she was away. "My ex-husband," she answered without the slightest hesitation. "He works the night shift so he comes home during the day to take care of the house. He lives two blocks away." They could afford to support two homes; in China one has to think twice before deciding to get a divorce, since it is extremely difficult to find a second place for one of the pair to live.

"Why did you divorce your husband?" I asked. "From what you've told me about him, he must be a nice guy." I had been in touch with Americans long enough not to feel too embarrassed to ask questions I would never have dared ask before.

"He is a nice person and he loves the girls, and he still loves me." Her voice was gentle and filled with affection. "We just didn't feel right together; so we talked about it and decided to get a divorce. But we see each other every day."

At this point her former husband, John, and her two daughters arrived at the doorway. It seemed John visited the family often. I wondered how he reacted when he saw her with other men. I would be jealous and would ask for remarriage. How could he restrain himself from holding on to this charming woman who was once his wife?

I liked the two girls. The face of the older one was lined with dirty sweat from playing in the grass, the younger one was sweet and quiet. I felt indignant with these selfish parents who apparently cared only about themselves. Many Chinese couples stay together for the sake of their children. Americans talk about the virtue of individualism, the value of freedom. They have, perhaps, too much narcississm in their individuality. Why don't they think a little more of their obligation to the children?

• • •

Among the Americans I met in Chicago, the Gardiners were the most "complete human beings" in the Chinese sense—compatible husband and wife, two lovely daughters of fifteen and thirteen who were not spoiled and not too "independent of" or "equal to" their parents. Their younger daughter, Carita, was just one year younger than my son. She was sweet and helpful to her parents, but she was still very much a child. I liked this family and liked going to their home.

Ron had written from Beijing to suggest that I get in touch with Judy and Richard Gardiner, but I hesitated to call them because I had no idea how they might react. Ron said that Judy was a teacher of English literature at Circle and that Richard was a doctor. When I did call, Judy answered the phone.

"We are having guests this weekend," she said. "I'll call you back next week." She was brisk and terse, and hung up. I immediately felt I was not welcome.

On Thursday of the following week, Judy called back. "Liu? Do you have anything to do this Saturday night? Good. Can you come to our house for dinner? Good. Richard will pick you up at seven. See you then." The phone clicked as she put down the receiver. So abrupt and matter-of-fact was the phone contact that I assumed the Gardiners would be somewhat aloof and that they were inviting me to dinner only because I knew Ron. I didn't really look forward to meeting them.

Both Richard and Judy turned out to be warmhearted people, each showing warmth in his and her own particular way. Richard showed it in his tone and words. Judy showed it in her smile and in the way she offered me food and drink—with earnest insistance, like a Chinese hostess.

The Gardiners had traveled to China as tourists in 1976, arriving in Beijing just when the earthquake occurred that destroyed the city of Tangshan. The earthquake woke them in the early morning in their hotel, and shortly afterwards, their guides had them packed and on their way to Shanghai. They didn't get a chance to see Beijing at all, but they were impressed by the concern the Chinese showed toward their safety and that of all the people in the affected areas.

Every three or four weeks, they would give me a call to ask if I wouldn't like to go out with them for dinner or to a movie, or come to their home. They didn't think the neighborhood was very safe and every time they would offer to pick me up, although I lived only three blocks away and passed their home every day on my way to and from school.

Ron and I were invited to Judy's fortieth birthday party,

which Richard had kept secret from her. At the party Judy was surprised and happy. I imagined how angry Fengyun would have been if I had spent as much money on wine and food without consulting with her. Richard explained to me, perhaps afraid I was thinking he was too extravagant, that they didn't do this often. "It is particularly for this occasion," he said. I understood; everyone has only one fortieth birthday to celebrate.

The party began with a short one-act play. I only understood the general idea, but it was about a primitive family that included a husband, played by Richard, a wife, played by a family friend, and a baby, all living peacefully in a prehistoric society. Several pots of flowers placed in front of them held signs reading "child care," "women's rights," "justice," and other words I've forgotten—all having personal meaning to this family. The Gardiners' two daughters, dressed in black robes, were the narrators. Then a patriarch dressed as a bishop came out and started to smash the flowerpots. Another evil figure appeared to fight the patriarch for power, while the primitive family huddled in the corner. Finally, a young woman with a red star in her hair and a ribbon bearing the word "socialista" over her shoulder came onstage and chased the oppressors away, then she revived the flowers. Everyone laughed.

After this, the guests danced to the Beatles music that had been playing when I arrived. Richard explained to me that most of the guests grew up with the Beatles' music, and it had a special meaning for them. The guests included the editor of *In These Times*, an independent socialist newspaper, and several professors who, I assumed, must be intellectuals and socialists like the Gardiners.

The girlfriend of a young professor from Circle persuaded me to dance with her. In Beijing, Ron had once wanted to take me to the International Club, an exclusive colony for foreigners where, among many cultural activities considered improper by the Chinese, they dance disco.

I declined his invitation because it was already after ten o'clock, a late hour for early-retiring Beijing residents, and Fengyun would be worried. My first contact with American dancing was when Jonathan, the son of my Evanston host, invited me to a rock-and-roll party. It was held in a bar crowded with three dozen young people, ranging in age from seventeen to twenty. The band was loud, the dancers jumped, shouted, kissed, embraced, cursed, and threw their hats, scarves and shoes toward the ceiling. Beer spilled onto the concrete floor; the smell of marijuana made me nauseous. I stayed for only twenty minutes, as a courtesy to Jonathan. Later, with my professional friends, I often went to parties that ended with dancing. The people at those parties danced with simple movements that anyone might learn in a matter of minutes; one just had to swing and twist to the beat of the music.

I asked Ron at Judy's birthday party if the guests were dancing disco. "Not exactly," he answered. "They dance the same step—their own—regardless of the music."

I danced several rounds, swinging awkwardly, still a little self-conscious, but not feeling a loss of dignity. American dancing no longer irritated me, and the Beatles songs were not so bad, either. It was good physical exercise and I felt relaxed.

One day Judy called to ask me to go with them to see the movie "Sunset" which starred the black comedian Richard Pryor. Though the audience, 80 percent black, laughed at his humor, I couldn't follow it. My mind was boggled by his indecent gestures and dirty remarks. I was also concerned about the impression he might be making on the youth and children in the audience. Viveta, the Gardiners' fifteen-year-old daughter, was seated next to me. For a time I considered asking the Gardiners if we should leave, but I realized that American youth are probably accustomed to such performances; even some of my Chinese roommates had visited an "adults only" movie house on Dearborn

Street to see just how decadent American culture might be. But I never wanted to do this. On our way home, both Richard and Judy apologized for taking me to such a low movie; they hadn't expected it to be so bad. "Never mind," I said. "It was worth it." This was the first time I had seen such a film, and I learned something. I had discovered a great deal about American standards by now, and few things shocked or surprised me anymore.

CHAPTER TWELVE

DAVID AND THE PAGAN

In the summer of 1981 I decided to look for a volunteer job, in the hope that by working with Americans I could get to know them better. My friend T. T. Chen of the U.S.-China Friendship Association recommended that I work at China Books where I would meet Americans interested in China. I volunteered two afternoons a week, doing little actual work there, but I did have a chance to talk a lot. On my way, I usually spent an hour or so in nearby Daley Center, where there were generally speeches, outdoor concerts, or other activities going on at noontime.

One day I was sitting near the fountain in Daley Center listening absentmindedly to a woman speaker from the Crusade for Christ movement. The June sun was comfortably warm, and the speaker's black accent was soothing to my ear. I lapsed into a doze. Suddenly, I sensed someone standing in front of me; I opened my eyes.

The stranger before me had blonde hair and a broad forehead. His short upper lip and slightly protruding front teeth gave him a sheepish expression, as if he had to make a special effort to close his mouth. He was about twenty-seven years old and was dressed in short sleeves and casual slacks.

"I am David Weidner," he said as he extended his hand to me. I started to rise, but before I could stand up, he was sitting beside me.

"Are you a Christian?" he asked. He had a thick voice that would be difficult for me to follow if he spoke fast. I was rather pleased that someone might take me for a Christian, because that meant my appearance wasn't so alien.

"No," I answered politely, "but I am reading the Bible." I wasn't lying. Even though I am an atheist, I had attended one of the Bible study classes given by four Christian groups on the Circle Campus. I couldn't understand the American culture if I knew nothing about the Bible, which is so much a part of this country's history and traditions. Furthermore, I thought understanding the language of the Bible might be important in my work as a translator. I was fascinated by many similarities between the stories in the Old Testament and those in Chinese legends. For example, in the Bible, when God got angry with man because of his corruption, God caused a deluge; in a Chinese tale, the Goddess who created man by kneading him out of earth got angry with man's greed and caused a huge flood. Also, many of the sayings attributed to Jesus express the same moral values as sayings of Confucius.

"One should put his faith in God," I heard David saying. "God tells us what to do and arranges our lives." He said something more that had little meaning to me. The sun was intoxicating. I fought back the habitual drowsiness I always felt around noontime. Chinese office workers have a long noon break in which to take a nap—an hour and a half in winter and two hours in summer. Here, I tried to westernize my habits, but this long-acquired drowsiness came punctually. I suppressed my yawns while David talked about how important it was to follow Jesus and how meaningless one's life is if one doesn't have faith in God. I remember asking him when he, himself, started to believe in God.

"I was raised a Christian," he said, "but I don't belong to any denomination. My belief is that we should do exactly what is written in the Bible."

I missed most of what David talked about for the next half hour. He talked with sincerity and patience, but I wondered why he exerted such efforts talking to a pagan like me. Was he trying to enlist a Chinese into his church? I was amused; either he was too naive to recognize who might really be a potential follower or he had the tenacity of a missionary working among savages.

I pitched in sporadically to impress him with my knowledge of the Bible as I had learned it. I told him I had read the book *Stories of the Bible* and Michener's novel *The Source*. But David, absorbed in his own preaching, was not impressed. From time to time he referred to an underlined passage or an annotation in the margin of his leather-covered Bible. His familiarity with this book was impressive.

When the speaker from the Crusade for Christ had ended her speech, a young man of David's same age came over to get him. David asked me if I would like to meet with him again. Of course I would; I gave him my address and telephone number, he left me his.

I had forgotten all about this encounter by the next week, when I received a telephone call from David. He had to remind me that we had met at Daley Center before I remembered who he was. I hadn't taken his offer to meet again seriously, since I had had too many such promises from casual acquaintances that never materialized.

We met at Daley Center again. Because it was drizzling, we went inside and sat on a crowded bench next to some shabbily dressed older people. David ignored all the hustle and bustle in the hall and talked to me about Matthew, the first Apostle. I felt uncomfortable in a public place reading verse by verse from the Bible, and I was keenly aware of the occasional glances from passersby. For more than an hour David and I talked, until finally I asked him if he would like to go across the street to a restaurant and have a drink. I ordered a beer and David had cocoa.

Afterwards we met once a week, usually at Daley Center. He told me he worked for the Northwest Church of Christ. One day, when it was too warm outside, David took me to the air-conditioned lounge of the Palmer House, where two waitresses served free ice cream to everyone. While David talked on and on, I grew nervous, as though I were sitting on a mattress sprinkled with needles.

After the weather turned cool in September, David drove to my place each week for our talks. There was good sunshine on our back porch in the afternoon, and there we sat, talking about the Bible. When the weather grew colder, my roommates and I could not afford to buy the enormous amount of oil the old oil furnace consumed, and we were tired of waiting for the landlord to convert it to gas. We left the heat off and our house became colder inside than out. A tiny room in the rear of the house had a small gas heater; I lit it and David and I continued our talks there, sitting on a broken bed.

Every time we met I found a few minutes to dig into David's personal life. Bit by bit, I learned that he was born in a small town midway between St. Louis and Chicago. His parents had a small farm nearby on which David grew up. He majored in theology at a college in Normal, Illinois, and moved to Chicago to work for the church. He was married and lived in a small house he owned on the far northwest side. He drove for twenty minutes to get to my place in order to have an hour's discussion—I felt ill at ease thinking of causing so much trouble for him.

"Not at all." David stopped my apology. "I enjoy speaking God's words to people." I was moved by his devotion.

I tried to ease my conscience by buying cans of soft drinks for him. Once, I cooked him a dozen Chinese dumplings for lunch when I learned he had not yet eaten. He ate the food without too much fuss or thanks. "That's delicious," was his only expression of appreciation.

I met Robin, David's wife, when she came with David to my house for a Bible lesson. She looked younger than David, and was a very pretty girl. Robin was already quite advanced in her pregnancy, and when David introduced her to me, he proudly remarked that it was certainly a wonder that God would form a baby out of nothing. The three of us went into the living room and sat on the sofa. David proceeded to ask Robin and me to read parts of a chapter of the Bible and, in turn, to discuss their significance. Robin, who knew the whole book by heart, read and answered David's questions like a pupil in a Chinese grade school. Listening to her, I wondered if American young people might not benefit greatly from a little more discipline, as she apparently had.

One sunny November day it was warm enough for us to sit on the back porch. Before David started the Bible lesson, he paused for a moment, then told me the church he worked for had decided to stop paying him, and he therefore had to look for a secular job. I was surprised to learn that a church may fire people. He was very disappointed at losing his church work, and I felt sorry, not so much because he had lost the chance to work directly for his God, but because of the worries he might have in finding another job.

"I don't worry. God will take care of me," David assured me. He bid me to open the Bible to Matthew, and he read: "Therefore I tell you, do not worry about your life, what you will eat or drink; or about your body, what you will wear... So do not worry, saying 'What shall we eat?' 'What shall we drink?' or 'What shall we wear?' For the pagans run after all these things, and your heavenly Father knows that you need them. But seek first His kingdom and His righteousness, and all these things will be given to you as well."

I thought to myself, yes, I am a pagan and I do seek all these things. I also realized David would no longer be coming to give me Bible lessons. He definitely wouldn't want to spend his own time and his own gasoline just to give me free Bible lessons. So I deliberately spent a little more time expressing my gratitude for the help he had given me in those months; it sounded like a farewell speech.

When David told me he would keep in touch with me and inform me of his job-hunting situation, I understood this to be a polite gesture. I was wrong. After he and Robin returned from a one-week vacation in Denver, he called me and arranged a meeting for another Bible lesson. He soon had a job as an associate manager of a new grocery store, and we continued to meet regularly until the summer when they moved away.

To some extent David and I developed a friendship outside of the subject of Jesus' teachings. He invited me to a baby shower, on a Saturday evening, given by the people from his church. I reluctantly agreed to stay at his house overnight and Saturday and go with him to church on Sunday morning. By Saturday noon when I hadn't received a call from David, I decided he had forgotten, and went downtown to visit a friend. I got home at 5:30 and found David at the door. He had been waiting outside since 4:30 reading his Bible. "It was too late last night when I remembered to call you," David said in his usual unhurried voice, "so I see I've caught you unprepared." He sounded so apologetic that I felt guilty for having wished he would not come.

The baby shower was held at a YMCA building where several people from David's church worked. People brought food for the adults and gifts for the unborn baby. The custom of celebrating a birth before the actual birth was new to me. In China we celebrate one month after a baby is born, and we call this the "celebration of the full moon." By that time, the mother is strong enough to move around, and the baby has gone through its most crucial period of survival. In the past the mortality rate among newborns was extremely high. The Chinese family often gives a banquet for close friends and relatives, and since the guests know by then if the baby is a boy or a girl, it is easier for them to select a gift.

About three dozen people came to David and Robin's baby shower. And I immediately noticed there were no black or other dark-skinned people. David introduced me to several young people and others came up to me. I asked what jobs they had. Mostly they were nonprofessional workers, such as carpenters, store clerks, or truck drivers. They were more openly curious about me than people I met at parties given by my professor or journalist friends. I was not as impressed by the many gifts for the baby as I was by the friendly atmosphere. There was a sense of closeness—brotherhood, as David and his religious friends called it—but also lack of intellectual sophistication.

I stayed overnight in David's neat, small house. The next morning Robin, moving heavily around the kitchen, prepared French toast for breakfast. At ten o'clock David, Robin and I drove fifteen minutes to the Lakeview Church of Christ. I asked David why he didn't go to a church nearer his home. He said he liked the way this church explained the Bible. I have yet to figure out why—since there's only one version of the Bible—there are so many Christian denominations. To me, all religions, like all political doctrines, have many high-sounding principles; but, in reality, these religions fight among themselves for secret, selfish interests.

Misunderstandings or not, I liked the atmosphere in the American churches I visited, especially the smaller ones. I didn't care much for the big churches where the people seemed remote and indifferent. I had been in the Catholic cathedral in the center of Beijing several times when I was working on an article in 1980 about the reopening of this church. It was large, seating at least a thousand people. The service was conducted in Latin, and I doubted that many Chinese churchgoers could follow it. That was my first contact with a church and it didn't leave me with a good impression.

After I came to the United States, I sometimes went to church with my religious friends. When I was in Missouri, I went to church with the Swisher family. Their's was a small, warm church where all the people knew each other. When the farmer reported to the congregation on my presence, they all turned in my direction and gave me welcome smiles. After the service, a dozen people came up to me to shake hands and to talk to me. I was glad to meet such friendly people.

David's church met in a small wood-frame house. I went with Robin to a room in the basement to attend the adult Bible class. David went off to another room to teach a group of teenagers. The teacher for the fourteen adults was an elder, who had been in charge of the baby shower the night before. He was lecturing on the book of Romans. The class responded to his questions with much greater eagerness than did students in the classrooms at Circle campus. Robin showed me the exercise book that everyone held. They had all done their homework. In the campus classes very often the students didn't do their reading assignments before class; in one class the professor asked how many students had read the chapter he had assigned—four out of thirty had. "See you tomorrow," the professor said as he picked up his books and left the room. The next day, six students didn't show up.

People who came to the Bible class were not seeking degrees and high-paying jobs. They came seeking the truth—something they might believe in. They could just as well have spent the morning at the beach, but they preferred to stay in that small basement room.

The elder stopped at Romans, chapter 14, verse 13: "Therefore let us stop passing judgment on one another. Instead, make up our mind not to put any stumbling block or obstacle in your brother's way." He asked for comments.

143

The class volunteered many explanations as to what a stumbling block or obstacle might be. Nobody, however, approached this question from a political point of view. It apparently never occurred to them that people now are not only putting stumbling blocks in other people's way for political reasons, but holding nuclear bombs over their brothers' heads. I looked around the small, packed room. From their clothes and manner I could tell these were lower-middle-class people, whose thoughts were not as complex as those of my professional friends. Their devoted, somewhat naive expressions led me to believe they could never represent a future world in which people would be brothers and sisters, as Jesus taught. Would we ever abandon all antagonisms and political disputes, or were they just dreaming of a world that had never and would never exist? Nevertheless, I was moved by their spirit and devotion.

David told me after we returned to his home that sometimes he felt uneasy owning a car and a house of his own. He wondered if these possessions prevented him from doing more for others, as his religion taught. I believed him and was grateful for the good things he had done for me; both David and Robin were nice people, yet I wasn't sure this was because of their natures or because of the teachings of Jesus in which they so firmly believed.

Chicago vaulted from winter to summer, with temperatures in the eighties in early May. David called me then and asked me to attend a Bible class at his home. I hesitated because I had had a full day—two classes in the morning and a paper I should work on that night. "Take a break," David said. He picked me up at seven that evening and drove me to his home. Sitting in his living room were nine people, all in their twenties.

David started the session by asking everyone to give an example of a time when or a reason why he or she felt trapped. First, a locksmith said he felt trappped by endless bills. Then, a warehouse worker said he felt trapped as if in a stuck elevator. Others gave examples of missing trains and groping in darkness to find the right direction.

When my turn came, I explained how my ambition to be best had trapped me in tension and frustration. One of the members of the group offered this advice to me: "Jesus said when you do something, do it with full mind and hand. That you want to be better than others is not a sin, as long as you don't do it for selfish ends."

The locksmith told me of a man who used a camping trailer to travel around the country after he retired. He lived simply and gave all he had saved to the needy. "Why have more money than you need?" he asked. "In this country there are too many temptations and it is easy to become a slave of money. People want more and more, but they will never find satisfaction with material things."

The discussion reminded me of another time when a friend had taken me to a Christian group meeting on the Northwestern campus in Evanston. More than fifty people, most of them in their early thirties, talked about the intensive competition in the world, about the me-generation, and about burn-out. When they asked what impression I had of American life, I said, "Americans have set a bad example for the world to follow. Because of their standards, people in other countries are learning to evaluate life only in terms of material possessions. They want to make more money and buy more things, as if life were nothing more than lust for personal pleasure. Over-industrialization everywhere may be detrimental to any genuine enjoyment in people's lives. It makes society function with the pace and sensitivity of a machine."

In the discussion that followed, I said that the telephone and television reduce human contact within the family, that highly mechanized office equipment and too much emphasis on efficiency restrict personal contact among colleagues. Someday, in the not-too-distant future, grocery orders will go out over cable television and people will just stay cooped up alone in their homes. Even now, to compensate for the lack of human warmth, Americans give and go to many parties, putting these dates on their calendars like appointments for departmental meetings. Because of all of this, I doubted whether the world was heading in the right direction. My point was warmly appreciated by the audience. After the meeting several people came over to shake my hand, saying as they did so, "Don't let your people become like us."

Of course I would like to tell my people, "Slow down. Haste doesn't make life any richer, only more complicated. Don't think too much of TV sets and refrigerators." But I doubt these words would make much sense to my people. The electronic era has brought some people enjoyable things, and the rest want these things too. Despite all the tension modernization is creating, most people think it is really wonderful. Though I talked at this meeting about the bad effects of a highly industrialized society, I, myself, wanted to take back from the United States a color TV set and a stereo—I obviously hand't gotten tired of them yet.

I had met people in the United States who were trying to simplify their lives. A retired professor planned to live in a country cottage and burn wood for cooking and heating. He asked me a lot about how Chinese farmers live in the villages and he thought he could live among them. In Madison, I met a chemical engineer who actually had given up such daily American necessities as a car, a telephone, a TV, and a refrigerator. He walked an hour each day to work, or miles to meet friends, or some distance to the store where he bought his daily groceries.

• • •

For several weeks I did not see David, and then he called me one day, late in June. "I went to New Mexico for a job interview at a church and was accepted," he said, sounding quite happy. "Can you come over Thursday afternoon to my house? We'll leave in two weeks and I hope we can see each other at least twice before then." Of course I could go to his house. I hadn't seen their newborn yet. I brought a little Chinese woolen dog for the baby.

David had been working long hours at his grocery store and was expecting a promotion soon, but he had not been satisfied with his work. "I wanted to work for the church again," he kept telling me. "I was too tied down to my job, with no time to think of God's words." He had been making a good salary, but more important to him was seeking peace of mind.

CHAPTER THIRTEEN

APARTMENT LIVING

In 1982 there were about 150 professors, lecturers and other professionals in the Chicago area who had all come to America not to enjoy material comforts but to seek opportunities to enrich our knowledge. But our ignorance of American life and our English skills were large obstacles in this new environment. Not only were we affected by the intense pace in the United States, but also by the pressures we brought to bear upon ourselves. Trying to make every minute of the stay worth the great personal sacrifice, many worked long hours in laboratories, returning to sparsely furnished apartments to read late into the night. Few of us took vacations or enjoyed any recreation. If we did travel, it was only to see and experience different parts of the country before we went home. We were mostly family men and women, unaccustomed to spending time away from our families.

Most of us had thought our English would improve quickly, but only after we had settled down and tried every means of communicating with Americans did we realize that it was not so simple. Some tried to live among

Americans, but they soon found the people here too busy with their social life to have time to talk. Perhaps if we had been twenty years younger, we might have lived in the dormitories and made more friends among the students.

We used every opportunity to speak just a couple of English sentences. One day, three of the scholars decided they would go out to talk to Americans. At first, they didn't know where to go—one couldn't just stop people on the street. They finally decided to go to the gymnasium on campus, where American students play table tennis. They stood around a table, watching the students playing. One scholar urged another to start talking, but no one had the courage to try. After ten minutes they returned home without having spoken a single English word. They tried many times to hold conversations in English between themselves; it felt so awkward, so foreign, they always reverted back to Chinese.

Like every other household of Chinese scholars, our's had a TV set and we watched the programs, not as much for the information as for the sounds of the language. Every evening we listened to the newscasters, who used standard English, and then later we could check what they had said against articles in the daily newspaper. At Circle each of us had weekly appointments at the Speech and Hearing Clinic to practice conversational English, though mostly, we worked and read by ourselves.

A foreigner living in China has to learn to speak Chinese very quickly if he or she wants to live among the Chinese, instead of in one of the special hotels for foreign residents. He has to tell the bus conductor his stop because the bus fare is charged according to distance. He has to name the item on the shelf behind the counter in a store so the salesman can get it for him. Sometimes the goods are under the counter, and if he doesn't know the name, the salesman won't understand what he wants.

Compared to this, living in the United States is easy. You

go into a store and take what you need from the shelves and put it into a shopping cart. Everything is in a package with the price marked on it. You pay the cashier as you leave the store. A novelty to me, at first, were eggs in plastic boxes—a dozen in each—so convenient, and we didn't need to worry about whether they might break or not. In China, we carefully lay eggs one by one into a basket when we buy them.

Sometimes I wondered if I would have had more chances for contacts with Americans if my family had been with me. Living with six middle-aged men under imposed bachelorhood did not offer many opportunities for entertaining American guests. Single men living together do not present *House Beautiful* surroundings.

● ● ●

By 1982, sixteen visiting Chinese scholars were enrolled at Circle, living in three groups near the campus. The six of us at 814 South Claremont, our tiny "Chinatown" as an American friend called it, shared all expenses and were fairly comfortable. But I often compared this life to the two years I spent in the labor reformation center. Here, also, I felt abandoned, and missed my family, always looking forward to Fengyun's letters. Even with plenty of food and material things available to me, I felt as empty as I did when I lived in the spartan barracks, surrounded by barren fields.

There the meals were so bad that the favorite subject was food, especially the fine meals we had had at Beijing restaurants. On long summer Sundays and cold winter nights, a few of the petty thieves would gather together and recall which restaurant had what tasty dish. There would be no end to these conversations which we called our "spiritual banquet." Everyone boasted about his experience, making it sound a hundred times more delectable than the real gourmet adventure. I detested such bragging, but I sometimes joined in to fill the emptiness in my heart (and stomach). I elaborated on the meals I had eaten in western-style restaurants where, in fact, I had only eaten a couple times with foreign colleagues. Later, others would take over my already blown-up story and tell it as their own.

The composition of our household had changed somewhat since I moved in. First, Yang Lidan and Xiao Liu transferred to a university in West Virginia, which agreed to pay them $800 and $600, respectively, for laboratory work. Compared to the $400-a-month government allowance we were getting, that sum was enviable. Then Zheng Zhenyi, dissatisfied with the cold attitude of his professor-sponsor at Circle, transferred to the University of Southern California. Margaret Shu, the Chinese-American nurse who rented an apartment in the rear part of our building, purchased a house in a suburb south of Chicago. We helped her move her belongings and get settled. Two recently arrived Chinese scholars moved into our vacated apartment, joining Zhao Jian and myself.

Soon thereafter, Zhao Jian began preparations to go home. With an English vocabulary barely broad enough to ask directions, Zhao had been the first Chinese visiting scholar at Circle campus in May 1980. "Arrival was awful," Zhao reminisced. "I came to Chicago alone and knew nobody. My heart beat faster as the plane was descending. What would my future be?" He was met by Professor Uslenghi who quickly spotted Zhao among all the other passengers by his appearance. He was conspicuous with his loose cut, 1940s style suit, in contrast to the tight-fitting American styles. China had more to catch up on than just technology and science. Professor Uslenghi drove him to Oak Park where he was to stay in the home of an elderly lady.

For two months Zhao lived in relative solitude, having no chance to make acquaintances with other Americans. During the day he went to school, sitting in a classroom but hardly knowing what the professor was talking about. He returned home in the afternoon to cook a simple supper in the basement kitchen and to lie on his bed.

He did meet some other Chinese, but they were from Hong Kong and Taiwan and were suspicious of this forty-three-year-old mainlander. Was he a Communist on some official mission? Some of them asked unfriendly questions. Those Taiwanese who were mainland sympathizers dared not talk to him openly at all, although some of them became bolder as relations between Beijing and Washington moved closer. They had been in the United States for many years and so were able to give Zhao and his roommate, Yang—both more than twenty years their senior—advice on how to cope with foreign life. These Taiwan students, and others who would later join them, became friends of the Chinese scholars; having the same ancestors and culture, there was a natural feeling of kinship.

Then Zhao received word that his father had died. He was tormented by the question of whether he should go home immediately or stay. He had not yet really begun his studies. If he went home now, the government would not likely send him out again. His wife urged him to stay and assured him she would take care of everything. Zhao stayed.

He was excited and relieved to learn that Yang Lidan, the second mainland scholar, would soon arrive. For the home they planned to make together, he rented a small apartment on South Claremont street, next door to the house we all lived in later. It was seven blocks west of the Circle campus. He bought pots and pans and found enough furniture for their needs.

By December 1980, Zheng Zhenyi, the computer researcher I had come to the United States with, expanded the mainland force on South Claremont to three. I found that Zheng was very capable and independent, a person I could rely upon. It was he I decided to live with later, when I could no longer stand the solitude of Medill and transferred to Circle.

Liang, a computer researcher from the Chinese Academy of Sciences, came to Chicago in June 1981. Being thrifty and meticulous, he soon became the quartermaster of our household. When he went to the super-market, he was content to pick out the lowest-priced items. I felt embarrassed buying only cheap things, but he seemed to care little what others might think. Without pretense, he said that what he wanted to do was to save money. Compared to him, I was vain and impractically proud: I felt the wealth of the United States belittled me; I was afraid of being unable to resist the temptations of this consumer society; I somewhat suspected that being from a poor country, I was looked down upon. Many of my Chinese friends shared the same feelings. If only China were strong and rich.

We shared the cooking by taking turns—a different cook each day. Actually, we only cooked dinner. For breakfast we each had a bowl of heated milk—we never got used to drinking cold milk. All but me carried a lunch—filling a plastic box with rice and leftovers from the last evening and reheating it in a microwave at the campus cafeteria. Going there was convenient and had the added benefit of providing us with free plastic spoons and napkins. The "cook on duty" came home early to prepare dinner. After a while, even those who had rarely cooked in China learned to prepare a couple of dishes.

Every two weeks we made a trip to the supermarket to buy groceries, usually on Friday, after checking the food advertisements in Thursday's newspaper. We made our purchases in bulk so that we could take advantage of the lower costs for larger quantities—twenty chickens at a time and thirty or forty pounds of oranges, when they were on sale. Because of the difference in diets between Chinese and Americans, the prices for some items worked to our advantage. For example, Americans don't like pork liver because it is high in cholesterol; pork liver is a delicacy to most Chinese. We bought at sixty cents a pound what would sell in Beijing for at least a dollar. Americans usually don't like to eat carp, considering it "dirty." since it eats along the bottom of the river. The first time I went to the fish market in Chicago, I was surprised to find fresh carp was selling at fifty cents a pound. We bought thirty pounds.

When we went to the supermarket we had to carry five or six heavy shopping bags home on the bus. One of us waited at the other end of the bus route with a shopping cart to help carry in the groceries. I found every excuse to be the one who waited at the bus stop; it was too much of an embarrassment for me to stand with a mountain of bags waiting for the bus outside the supermarket, watching other people taking their bags home in cars. In the United States I was constantly aware of being without material things. In Beijing I never thought about owning a car and never felt inconvenienced by not having one. A bicycle there is a most handy means of transportation, and I could go everywhere on one.

"We were like a bunch of pathetic fools at the bus stop," Young Xue, a physics engineer, said to me after he got off the bus with six shopping bags. "The Americans must be thinking, 'these poor Chinese'," he joked bitterly as we dragged the loaded cart along the sidewalk that was covered with seven inches of snow. We wouldn't have felt this way dragging a cartload of groceries along a street in Beijing—everybody there does the same thing.

Zhang Chi, one of my roommates, who was nearly fifty, didn't know much about cooking when he first joined us; however, he took his turn at cooking once a week. Very soon he developed a marvelous specialty; being artistic, he took the responsibility for preparing and arranging the cold hors d'oeuvre platter that we served when we had special guests. We entertained our teachers and Taiwan friends sometimes, but only those we were close to. On such occasions, everyone cooked a couple of dishes, and our guests were always surprised to see how well we did.

Of course we all knew how to cook since every husband cooks and does household chores in China. All of us were in our forties and grew up in a period when the Chinese government took an active part in promoting the advancement of women's rights and equality. In order to follow the ancient Chinese principle "To exceed the proper limits in righting a wrong," the government urged men to show special respect for women.

In present Chinese society, there are three different views of the role of women, held by three rather distinct age groups. Those over fifty place the highest value on old traditions of men doing the heavy household work while women attend to the household chores. Those in my age bracket, thirty-five to fifty, have a different opinion. After 1949, when the new government was founded, all young girls began to go to school; thus, our wives have the same kind of jobs and salary that we do, so we share the household work. After office hours my wife and I hurry home, buying groceries along the way, and prepare the dinner together. I actually do more of the cooking than Fengyun does when we entertain guests. The third group is made up of those under thirty, the sexually liberated ones who are outwardly open in expressions of affection and who take equality between men and women for granted. More and more, these persons are influenced by western attitudes toward relationships.

• • •

Over the supper table in our Claremont house, we talked about our plans after going home. Many wanted to take vacation trips in China with their families. Such a pastime had never occurred to us before we came to the United States. Traveling was a new way of life we learned from Americans, who adore traveling far and wide over the world. Even when we had vacations in China, we had no money to travel. Only those who worked far from their families were given time each year to go home, their travel expenses paid by their working units.

To fill the emptiness of our lives, we often talked about

155

our imaginary vacations, a kind of "spiritual banquet" not unlike the kind I had in the labor reformation center. Many of our wives would have perhaps hated to spend three or four hundred yuan just "playing with mountains and rivers," preferring to spend the money to buy nice clothes. But just talking about something that brought our families to the scene helped ease the loneliness of life in America.

Another favorite "dish" at our "spiritual banquet" was thinking about what things we would take home. The first big item Chinese purchased was a good-quality camera in order to take dozens of pictures to send home. This was bought usually within a matter of three months after arrival, when enough money had been saved. The great variety of cameras, TV sets, stereos and other electronic toys in the United States are much cheaper than in China. Though $400 a month is not much, each of us could manage to save enough to buy and take back the allowed quantity of duty-free items. We would not have been able to afford such things had we saved for a lifetime in China.

• • •

The winter of 1981-1982 was long and bitter. After the last snow in mid-April, the temperature struggled up to above 50 and then dropped again to the mid-30s; it lingered at 50 for a week and suddenly jumped within three days to nearly 80, when we shut off the furnace for the summer. But during the cold February and March months, our gas bills had run to $270 a month, heating the poorly insulated house to only 60 degrees. The others went to their laboratories or offices during the day, taking lunch with them. I went to two classes in the morning and came home to the cold house at noon. With a plate of quickly prepared fried rice or noodles on my lap, I watched the noon news on television and then the soap opera "Days of Our Lives." This program is an endless series of seemingly all-American beautiful women and handsome men who don't know whom they should seriously love so they sleep around a lot.

The superficial characters and insipid plot are consistent with the program's theme, "Like sand through the hourglass, so are the days of our lives."

By the time the program ended, the sun had passed its zenith and filled the back porch overlooking the courtyard with sunshine. I would take a chair out and read and write. Either because the winter of 1980-1981 had been mild or because then I was constantly in a low mood, I hadn't noticed the beauty of the peaceful surroundings of our little house on South Claremont.

One block east was busy Western Avenue, but on our quiet, one-way street hardly a dozen cars went by in an afternoon. Several streets east of ours was an old Italian neighborhood, said to have survived the 1871 Chicago Fire. People were talking about restoring this part of the city as an historic site. "The property value will go up soon," our landlord said. "I'll remodel this house and rent it to a doctor for $1,000 a month." But I saw Italians moving out of the neighborhood and Mexicans moving in. That meant the property values would soon go down.

The trees, especially several flowering ones that had burst into pink blossoms overnight, decorated our street and enhanced the peacefulness. I watched a bush outside my window growing thicker, budding, and blossoming into tiny yellow flowers in a span of only five days, when the temperature rose from the freezing point to more than 70 degrees. Without my knowing it, the tulips on the terrace had already put out blazing red and snowy white flowers.

The grass had been green since the last patch of snow melted, but it needed care. Three or four species of birds hopped on the ground, picking among dead leaves, singing and jumping in the bushes along the fence. Two or three squirrels must have had a nest nearby since I often saw them scurrying up and down the big tree in the middle of the yard.

While I was sitting on the back porch, feeling as though I

owned the whole world, my mind often drifted. What would it be like if Fengyun and our son were living in this house? Surely we wouldn't neglect or waste such a big yard. We would not wait for the weather to turn warm to dig up a corner and plant a vegetable garden. Last spring I had thought of planting some vegetables; since I had worked in a vegetable garden before, it wouldn't have been too difficult to grow peppers, tomatoes, and cucumbers. I talked about this several times, but was unable to get myself into the mood to start the project.

Fengyun brings earth up thirteen floors from a nearby park, in order to plant flowers in the several pots she keeps in our apartment. She loves flowers and would be overjoyed to have such a spot of land where she could plant them. But I knew she wouldn't like to live in a foreign country. She is as traditionally Chinese as I am.

The house and the yard needed more care. A friend of mine who owned an apartment building visited us one day, looked around at the needed repairs, and commented that we seemed to have a bad landlord. About my age, our landlord, Frank, worked for the Circle campus Security Office as a policeman and seldom came to inspect his property. He let the beautiful courtyard go to waste, leaving all the clean-up work for us to do. Since we didn't know that this was a landlord's job, we raked up the dead leaves in the yard so the grass would grow, and cleaned out the basement when the weather turned warm to keep it from smelling.

Because we wanted to be on good terms with him, we invited him and his girlfriend over for a nice dinner. And when he was replacing the old oil furnace with a gas heater, I assisted him on many afternoons. On the two record cold days, when all the pipes froze, he came out when we called and put a hot line along the water pipes. We then had water all right, but the pipes to the washbasin in the bathroom and the pipe to the sink in the basement remained clogged. We telephoned him repeatedly, but he was never at home, perhaps spending most of his off-duty time with his girlfriend.

The most terrible problem through the winter was rats. I never saw such big rats in China—they chewed on everything. We tried to hide everything from them by hanging our rice bag from the ceiling and putting all leftover food immediately into the refrigerator. One night the person on duty forgot to put the dishes away, and after half an hour when he came back downstairs, he found the dishes on the table as clean as if they had been licked by a dog. But they had been licked by rats. "Americans have a lot of food," one of my roommates joked. "These rats are lucky to be born in the United States."

We didn't know where the rats came from until one afternoon, as I was sitting on the back porch reading, I heard a scurrying noise and saw a huge rat rummaging under the wooden stairs of the garage. Outside the garage, there were three big garbage bins. The rats must have been living in the garage, then moved into our basement when it got cold. American friends urged us to report the problem to the city government. We didn't do so because that would embarrass our landlord; instead, I wrote a note to him and enclosed it along with the rent check.

Dear Frank,

We tried to contact you on the phone. You didn't answer. So with the check we are sending you a note.

You promised to clean the basement, but until now you haven't done anything. And the conditions there were terrible. Six of us spent a whole Sunday afternoon getting rid of all the garbage. We also moved all your tools and stuff from the small rear room behind the kitchen to the basement. We pay for that room too, but it has been taken up by your tools for four months.

The sink pipes in the bathroom and in the

basement are still clogged. Could you please do something?

The most important matter we want you to attend to is the RATS. We cannot "coexist" with them any longer. We killed a few in traps, but the older ones are too smart to get caught. They chew our clothes; one pair of leather shoes and a new sweater are damaged. Our American friends urge us to report this to the city. We haven't done so, because we think you can deal with the problem.

Hope to see you soon.

Tenants at 814 S. Claremont

I felt I was very brave to write such a note. Frank didn't show up until nearly a month later, when the boiler broke down. All the rats except the biggest one left when the weather warmed up. We didn't report anything to the city as we threatened.

After all, Frank was a nice guy in his own way. When Zhao Jian, Yang Lidan and Zheng Zhenyi, the first three Chinese visiting scholars at Circle, moved from the small apartment in Frank's three-flat building next door into this much larger house, he hadn't asked them to pay additional $100 deposits. When we took over the rear part of the second floor, he didn't ask for deposits at all. When the cold weather set in, he spent $6,000 to replace the old oil furnace with a gas heater and worked on the installation for many days. This saved us some money on heating bills. And when we had more people move in and needed extra beds, he bought two new ones for us.

Frank might have been taking advantage of us Chinese, who knew next to nothing about the landlord-tenant relationship. And he also might have been as ignorant as we were about owning property, but anyway, we got along well and never had an argument.

CHAPTER FOURTEEN

THE CABIN IN THE WOODS

The two Chinese characters for the words "United States" literally translate as "Beautiful Country." Although I had been in Washington with its grand museums and Capitol Hill, in St. Louis where the Mississippi flows, in Madison and in Milwaukee, I really felt the beauty of this country was in places like the farm in Marshall, Missouri, and the forest preserve in Glencoe, Illinois. Many times I was on fabulous Lake Shore Drive along Lake Michigan in Chicago, with its exclusive condominiums and expensive shops, but this did not impress me. From the top of the Sears Tower in Chicago I had seen the dirty, hazy skyline and gray sprawl of the city, the miniature cars, toylike trains, and people like ants milling around and struggling to grow old. All of this had convinced me only more that the beauty of the United States lies in the land that has not been gashed and spoiled by people.

I was again going to have the opportunity to go out into the countryside and enjoy this beauty. May Kay Hobbs, the director of the Center for Teaching about China, had asked me to spend the Memorial Day weekend with her at her parents' summer house in northern Wisconsin. We were going to swim and canoe, so we needed good weather. It had seemed that Chicago wouldn't have a spring in 1982. The temperature jumped from the mid-40s at the end of April to the 80s in early May, and then back into the 60s in mid-May. Temperature records were set and the sky was always overcast.

The weekend turned out to be perfect. By May 28 it was 75 degrees under clear blue skies. At one o'clock Mary Kay, and a Chinese student who was staying at her house, picked me up and we began to drive north. Because Mary Kay had recently gotten her Ph.D. in Chinese studies, we spent the first two hours of the car ride talking about China. After we passed Milwaukee, the view of woods and fields along Highway 45 was quite breathtaking.

Two hours north from Milwaukee, the woods along the highway became denser and wilder, with no more great stretches of open, bare fields. The traffic was heavy with vacationers, many towing campers and motorboats. Road signs with a picture of a deer reminded speeding drivers to watch out for the deer that sometimes jump across the highways in Wisconsin; Mary Kay told me there were also bears in the woods. I was eager to see deer in the wild, but saw only two that must have been killed by cars in the early morning, when deer are most active.

I told Mary Kay that deer meat is delicious. I had never eaten any, but I remembered that in a chapter of the famous sixteenth-century Chinese novel *Dream of Red Mansions* I had read a vivid description about how tasty barbecued deer meat is. I described the story to Mary Kay, hinting that I would like to take one of the slain deer home. She didn't get my hint, and we drove on. What a waste of food! I was thinking.

After we passed Indigo, a small town in northern Wisconsin, we left Highway 45. The other vacationers also turned down narrow country roads, heading for different lakes. The woods merged into forests of birch, poplar and pine. Half an hour before we reached Upper Post Lake, our destination, a little rain fell, shrouding the forest in haze. Mary Kay explained to me the meaning of French and Indian names for the towns, the area, and the roads. She pointed to where a bloody battle had been fought between French settlers and Indians, and to where the British army had maintained a post to keep the Indians in check.

I saw a sign reading "Indian Crafts Store." Mary Kay told me a white woman was running this store, but that she knew nothing about what she sold. She asked me if I wanted to stop. I said no, I had visited the Natural History Museum in Washington, where I had seen dioramas of Indians "living" in miniature tepees and caves. Here, I told her, I would like to meet live Indians.

North of Milwaukee we passed through several more towns on our seven-hour drive and I didn't see any other skin color there but white. People in northern Wisconsin, descendants of German and Scandinavian immigrants, generally have blonde hair and fair skin, and they are sturdily built.

"Where are the Indians?" I asked.

"They are on reservations to the west," Mary Kay told me.

In Madison my friends had taken me to a forest preserve and, pointing out a great mound in the midst of the trees, told me it was an Indian burial ground. Wisconsin used to have great numbers of Indians. I didn't meet any there, but I heard legends about them and saw Indian souvenirs sold by white people. As we continued our drive, my imagination ran wild into the forests stretching east and west from the highway. No more than a hundred years ago herds of buffalo and solitary moose roamed over this wild land.

Occasionally we passed breaks in the forest, and small farms appeared. The land here was not as rich as that to the south, but it still produced good crops. I have seen crops on much worse land in many parts of China. Such forest areas as this would have been leveled for crops a thousand years ago in China. "Imagine," I wondered aloud, half to myself and half for the benefit of Mary Kay, "What would happen if the United States had five or six hundred million more people? Could you keep these trees here?"

Mary Kay laughed, "I don't know," she said.

I saw a skunk, then a woodchuck, lying at the side of the road, apparently struck by cars. Patches of scarlet flowers, then patches of white flowers dotted the woods. After the long but pleasant drive, we arrived at Mary Kay's parents' house just before dusk. Mr. and Mrs. Hobbs greeted us most cordially.

The cabin, as Mr. Hobbs called it, stood on the edge of Upper Post Lake. Along the side of this lake were many cottages like Mr. Hobb's, most of them screened by trees. In front of each house was a lawn or vegetable garden; an asphalt road surrounded the lake like a girdle. On the opposite side of the lake I saw only a few houses. Most of the people living there had built their own cottages. Apparently it is quite easy, with all the wood available; they simply buy prefabricated materials and assemble them.

Mr. Hobbs pointed to five tall pine trees, remnants of the original forest which had been too young to cut down when the area was cleared ten years ago. He said that now 80 percent of the forest was owned by private individuals who had the right to cut the trees and turn the land into crop fields. He also explained to me the history of this now booming community. "Fifteen years ago, there was not even a road here," he said, "and ten years ago I was the first on this side of the lake to buy a spot to build this cabin on. I did most of the work myself, hiring people only to sink a well and to string the electric lines. The whole thing cost me $1,200. Now it would cost many times that."

I went with Mr. Hobbs into his forest and trimmed trees. I fished on the lake and canoed after dark, when there were only two or three other boats out. I roamed along the edge of the forest and wished I had the courage to disappear into the trees and live as a wild man. But I did encounter signs reading "No Trespassing" and "Beware of Dogs."

• • •

Mr. Hobbs, a seventy-six-year-old retired minister, became rather philosophical as we sat in his living room overlooking the lake. We were talking about Indians.

"White people believe in conquering nature," he said. "Indians believe in living with nature. When they kill an animal, they go through an elaborate ritual of prayer to their gods about killing the animal for food. They say that plowing the land is like gashing your mother's belly." He told me a story about an Indian tribe that sold a stretch of land to white people. The white people built houses on the land and grew crops. After seeing them do this, the Indians returned to demand back their land. The land belongs to everyone, they said, and tore down the houses. "They don't understand the meaning of ownership," Mr. Hobbs said, "and they don't understand accumulation of wealth."

I asked him if it would change the Indians' attitudes to educate them. His answer was that some Indian students go out to get an education, but they always return to live on their reservations."

Judy, the professor at Circle's Speech and Hearing Clinic, had told me that Circle once had a program for teaching Indian students. The students didn't ask questions and wouldn't look straight at the professors; they believed that staring meant disrespect. They didn't have enough people on the staff who understood the Indians, so the Circle program was stopped after a year.

I asked Mr. Hobbs if there would soon be a town in this Upper Post Lake area. "They are talking about putting in sewage and water supply systems here," he replied, "and they say the area has a rich deposit of zinc ore."

Mrs. Hobbs, patiently working on a needlework picture of two robins, added, "A company wants to mine the zinc.

Fortunately, Wisconsin has strict regulations that require anyone who wants to mine to pay a lot of money, but I think the company will eventually do so. For now, they prefer to open mines in Canada."

• • •

During the few days I lived by the lake, I came to realize something I had only vaguely felt before—a subconscious need to be with nature. Didn't I always want to go to the fields instead of crowded parks in Beijing? Didn't I always feel indifferent to the big cities? I realized now why I was not interested in seeing great cities such as New York and San Francisco which my American friends tried to persuade me to visit. These cities, I believed, would be no different from one another, nothing more than high buildings, department stores, and great museums which display live or mummified specimens. I had liked my stay on the Missouri farm because I had felt close to what was natural and alive. Here, in northern Wisconsin, I was feeling even closer to nature.

Many of the summer dwellers on Upper Post Lake were retired. The Hobbses' elderly neighbor, a lumber worker in a plywood factory at Indigo—fifty miles south of the lake— was planning to retire within two years. On the last morning of our stay, I talked with him while he leveled some ground for the garage he was building. He was quite interested in the life we lead in China. I told him how lucky he and other Americans were to have so much space. "I would like to see China with some of the forests you have here," I said. "Our forests are found only in remote mountain areas; we have turned most of our land into fields that can give us crops." He had not realized how crowded our land was.

These older people must have gotten tired of the noisy world and of competing with one another for fame and profit. At their advanced ages, the desire to communicate with nature had led them to find this place. I have seen only one person die—my mother. As she was dying, she kept trying to put her feet on the floor. We prevented this by lifting her feet to the "proper position" on the bed. An old lady in our courtyard later told me that my mother had wanted to return to Mother Earth. I think I can now understand why.

After three days of living in the woods, we drove back toward Chicago in a stream of cars. By the side of the road I counted four dead deer, killed by cars that very morning.

CHAPTER FIFTEEN

MAINLANDERS, TAIWANESE, AND CHINESE-AMERICANS

I had been so absorbed in my studies of American life and language that I never took the time to go out with my Chinese roommates to a movie or to a park. During the seventeen months in Chicago I went with them only twice, to the lakeshore. I had made more and more American friends and was involved with them in social events, visits, and short trips. When my Chinese friends made plans for a weekend, they stopped counting me in their group. Some, both the Chinese visiting scholars and a few Chinese from Taiwan that I knew casually, had begun saying that I was a busy man in American society—I sensed their sarcasm. They were probably thinking that I considered it beneath my "dignity" to go out with them. I felt somewhat guilty about this.

The Fourth of July was coming up, and by now, I had decided to go back to China in mid-September, no longer able to stand a wanderer's life; this was two and a half months short of my two-year plan. I was therefore determined to spend more time with my Chinese compatriots. I declined a couple of invitations from my

American friends for get-togethers on the Fourth of July holiday, and declared weeks ahead that I was going to go with my roommates to Grant Park to see the celebrations. We planned to have a picnic, then watch the annual fireworks. Our quartermaster, Liang, had bought drinks and food for the occasion.

The Fourth of July was on Sunday, but the pragmatic Americans had decided that Saturday night would be more convenient for the fireworks and so they had programmed the major activities for then. On Saturday night we were watching television when a friend living four houses away came in and asked if we had heard about the change; it was already a quarter past nine. To confirm this news, Zhou, one of my roommates, called Judy, the professor at the Speech and Hearing Clinic from whom we often solicited such help. She said yes, the fireworks were that night.

We set out after five minutes of hesitation, discussing whether it was worthwhile to go out so late. I was for it, still quite eager to follow through on our holiday plan. Out we went, seven of us—five from my house and two from the other. I told Liang, who was reluctant to go at such a late hour, how magnificent the changing lights on Buckingham Fountain would be; we literally dragged him along.

The scene at Grant Park was not much different from the one I had seen the year before with several Americans from the U.S.-China People's Friendship Association: crowds, paper plates, plastic beer cups, and food stands. People waited in long lines to buy a cup of beer or to go to the bathroom. We regretted not having brought drinks with us. I noticed a phenomenon that was lacking the previous Fourth of July—Chinese firecrackers. They were exploding in every corner, adding a new flavor to this celebration, the biggest public festival in the United States. Kids and young men threw firecrackers into the crowd. The tiny hissing packages of dynamite burst at people's feet, behind their backs, and over their heads, sending girls jumping and shrieking. Big ones boomed, little ones cracked. A pungent fragrance filled the air.

We squeezed forward to the waterfront to watch the public fireworks over the lake. The whole sky was filled with dazzling colors. The fireworks were beautiful, especially when they were reflected in the water, but they were not as magnificent as those I had often seen in Beijing on China's National Day. People cheered and applauded as each pattern spread out in the dark blue sky; their faces were open, their smiles genuine. I like the spontaneity with which Americans express their feelings. Chinese would be too embarrassed to let out such unchecked shouts of joy in a crowded place.

The fountain lights disappointed me, however. They remained one color: dim amber. Since many public programs were being cut due to the slowdown in the economy of the United States, I wondered if finances for operating Buckingham Fountain had also been reduced.

At 11:30, the fireworks display now over, we returned to the fountain, hoping to catch some of its color changes. One previous summer night I had stood there for forty minutes counting how many patterns the colored lights could make—I had lost count. But now even the amber lights were gone, leaving the dark contour of the fountain tinged by the glow from building lights on Michigan Avenue. Many people standing around us also seemed disappointed at not seeing the lights.

I told my friends, "Wait a little while—they are having mechanical trouble with the lights and surely are repairing them. Since there are so many people waiting, the lights will certainly come on very soon." I was eager to placate the complaining Liang, who was saying that we had wasted a whole evening. I began to regret having urged him to come that night.

The park officials were, indeed, having trouble, not with the equipment but with a human being. On the second tier of the fountain, a naked white body was moving around under the edge of the third and top tier, groping for a way to pull himself up onto it. Obviously, the top tier was too high for him to reach and he made hopeless gestures toward the agitated crowd. He then seemed to give up his goal and began to put his pants on. The crowd shouted, "Don't give up!" "Go for it!" I was fascinated that several young women joined in the chorus of cheering, as if afraid the naked man would be gone and they could enjoy the scene no longer.

Finally the figure in the fountain found a ladder. As he placed it against the edge of the third tier and climbed triumphantly on top of it, cheers burst out; women whistled and men laughed. The figure stretched his white arms to the sky and paraded around the top tier triumphantly, displaying his nude body in the shimmering lights from Michigan Avenue. Someone tried to photograph the scene, probably to sell to a newspaper, I thought.

The figure stayed there for twenty minutes as the crowd cheered. Policemen, two dozen in all, surrounded the inner ring of the fountain, and I heard some people from the crowd call them "pigs." When they finally persuaded the man to come down and he was being led away by the police, the crowd began to chant, "Let 'im go! Let 'im go!"

The previous November, a man had illegally climbed the John Hancock Building. He won a great deal of publicity in the newspapers and on television; someone even paid his fifty thousand dollar fine. I was therefore surprised to see no account of this nude Buckingham Fountain climber in the press. Perhaps it was too dark, and so no one was lucky enough to get a clear photograph of him. Five days later, the *Chicago Tribune* reported that a woman, forty years of age, had walked naked along North Michigan Avenue in the middle of the day, causing a twenty-minute traffic jam.

• • •

I felt the temperature rising as I went to bed that Saturday night after returning from Grant Park. The kids in the street were still setting off firecrackers and rockets, and their stereo was blasting out rock-and-roll music. Our window glass rattled. Rock and roll and Chinese firecrackers, both loud and noisy, brought the cultures of West and East into an exotic, but not so harmonious, combination.

The next day broke hot. The kids opened the hydrant on the street corner to full blast, as they had the summer before; gallons of water poured out and flowed into the gutter. I knew that in Beijing the residents were doing everything they could think of to save water.

At noon Lin and Zhang, two women students from Taiwan, came to meet me so that we could go together to a picnic with Dr. Liu and his wife. They drove me to Dr. Liu's house in the northern suburb of Wilmette. Joining us were a Chinese woman from the mainland, who was studying under Dr. Liu, and a Chinese visiting doctor. I had been to Dr. Liu's house three times before, and had met some of his American, Japanese, Filipino and Korean friends. Like other Chinese living in the northern suburbs of Chicago, the doctor owned a house worth hundreds of thousands of dollars. He had a neatly kept lawn and a backyard with flowers. There was one car parked in front of the garage and another one inside.

From Dr. Liu's house we drove to a forest preserve by a lake for our picnic. In this lovely atmosphere we talked and relaxed and ate American food—barbecued hamburgers, chicken and hot dogs. I enjoyed being among all Chinese, speaking only Chinese, feeling the comfort of being with my own people.

Living in an expensive northern suburb of Chicago meant a higher social status and a better education for Dr. Liu's children. His family, like other Chinese families in the northern suburbs, had little contact with the merchant Chinese in Chicago's Chinatown. The residents of Chinatown traced their origins mostly to Canton or its neighboring counties. Many were descended from laborers. They didn't trust outsiders, and the Chinese they spoke was more foreign to me than English. The only contacts I had with them were during a few dinners I had with American friends in Chinese restaurants there.

The differences between the Chinatown Chinese and Chinese from other places were not simply due to geography. There is a long tradition in China that intellectuals hold contempt for merchants. In old China, people were categorized in this order: scholars, farmers, workers, and merchants; the last were at the bottom of Chinese society, no matter how much wealth they had.

Quite a few successful Chinese residents—professionals and businessmen with higher education—lived in the wealthy suburbs of Skokie, Evanston and Wilmette. They had little contact with each other in the sense of a Chinese community. Some were supporters of the mainland, and some of Taiwan; most of them supported neither—putting feet on two boats, as the Chinese saying goes.

The most successful Chinese I had met in Chicago was Dr. Wang, a plastic surgeon. With a degree from a Chinese medical college, he had come to the United States in 1946. He studied and passed the U.S. medical exams to obtain his medical license; after a few years, he opened his own practice and continued to work in a hospital. He married his American assistant, had a daughter and then a son. Over sixty now, he is still doing surgery and earns a great deal of money. One evening, he invited all Chinese visiting scholars at Circle to have dinner with his family in Chinatown. On China's National Day, October 1, 1981, he treated nearly a hundred Chinese visiting scholars in the Chicago area to a celebration dinner.

In Chinatown, almost all the children speak Chinese, while the children of these affluent Chinese in northern suburbs speak only English. The first time I went to Dr.

Liu's house, his nineteen-year-old son was there. Dr. Liu didn't introduce me to him, as is the custom in a Chinese family receiving guests. And this time at his house I had seen his younger daughter. She was in the kitchen watching television and didn't come into the living room to greet us. I knew she didn't speak Chinese, as was the case with many ABCs—American Born Chinese—since their parents don't encourage them to do so. The reason, one Chinese professor told me, is because the competition in suburban schools is so great that they want their children to devote all their energy to American schoolwork. An interesting point is that many of these Chinese children later take Chinese language and history courses in college to offset what they missed in their family education.

At one Chinese professor's house I talked to his two sons, ages twelve and fifteen. They showed me how to play video games on the computer their father had recently bought for them. "They didn't want to play with me," the younger one said of his white classmates, speaking English without the slightest trace of an accent. "But, after my dad bought this for me, they wanted to come to our house all the time. But I don't give a damn whether they come or not." I knew, of course, that he cared very much. That evening, the two sons were quite happy because I played table tennis with them for an hour in their basement, which was filled with all sorts of recreation facilities. At the dinner table, however, they were not seen; they ate in their own room, away from the conversation conducted in Chinese between the guests and their parents.

I went twice to the Skokie home of a Chinese couple whose English was no better than mine. Their college-age son and daughter didn't speak any Chinese either. While we were talking and eating in the living room, the two youths watched TV and read in the basement.

At the picnic Lin and I discussed this difference between suburban and Chinatown Chinese children. In Chinatown, children went to elementary school with many Chinese classmates. After school, they took special classes taught in Chinese. I remarked that this was sensible. "That's why they don't speak good English," Lin said.

Lin and Zhang, and Shen—who did not come along today—were the only Taiwan students I knew well enough to call friends while I was at Circle. All of them were in their late twenties and were working on their Ph.D's. They had lived together in the school dormitory for nearly two years.

I asked Zhang, a delicate and petite woman who was quite well read, if she wanted to go back to Taiwan. "There are too many people in Taiwan," she said. "It is difficult to find a job there, especially in the field I am studying." She was in the field of sociology and had just published her master's thesis. She had earlier been a student at Cambridge, in the field of archaeology. I had read a few pages of her thesis and marveled at her knowledge of ancient Chinese culture. I wondered why she was in the United States conducting research on things Chinese.

"I would prefer a job in Taiwan," she said. "Every year I check with my folks to see if there is a place for me, but I don't have the right contacts. Meanwhile, my folks are expecting me to achieve something in the United States—I can't go back like this." She lived on about five hundred dollars a month as a teaching assistant.

Lin was writing her Ph.D. dissertation on how senior Chinese-Americans feel living in the United States. "I find it easy to live in the United States," Lin said. "For the past five years I have been at Circle, first as a teaching assistant and later working part-time for Dr. Liu." She was much better off than Zhang or Shen. Two years ago she had gotten her green card which permitted her to work in America. In another three years she would be an American citizen. Most of her family members—mother, brother and two sisters—were in the United States. Her father in Taiwan had a good job and didn't want to give it up. "I want to go to work or teach on the mainland for a few years," she said, "but I won't go there until I have my Ph.D. and have become an American." I understood.

Lin, nearly thirty (an old maid by Chinese standards), thought of herself as a career woman. She was looking for a new boyfriend. "Many American women don't marry," she said.

"You are taking to the American taste." I joked. "How does it feel?"

"My mother always asks when I am going to marry, and what boyfriend I have, but I don't like to talk to her about it. I had a boyfriend, but when he wanted me to move to San Francisco and live with his mother, we split. His mother is old-fashioned; she wanted me to stay home and cook."

On the few occasions when the three women from Taiwan and I got together, we talked about China. We hoped that China and Taiwan would eventually end their hostilities and join together to make China strong. Taiwan has a surplus of college graduates, while the mainland is short of them. Two-thirds of the Taiwan students in the United States remain after they get their degrees. What a shame Chinese minds cannot serve the Chinese nation.

I had no contact with Hong Kong students. From what I learned from others, the Hong Kong students felt homeless; they didn't want to go to either the mainland or Taiwan. "There are too many differences and I don't think I could feel comfortable," one of them told one of my roommates. Yet they were not, and perhaps never would be, satisfied with the lives they had in the United States.

At a 1981 Asian-American conference in Chicago, a Japanese-American scholar reported that the third and fourth-generation Japanese descendants in the United States typically identified themselves as American citizens, and didn't want to be referred to as Japanese. I was glad to get a chance to check the validity of this statement when Russell, a medical student, took me to a Japanese-American-sponsored concert at Northwestern Univesity in Evanston. Two-thirds of the audience were Japanese, and Russell knew some of them. After the concert he asked three young Japanese, a man and two women, to go out with us for a bite to eat. This was the first time I had sat down with young Japanese-Americans and what the scholar had said at the conference was fresh on my mind. The two Japanese women were *sansei* (third generation). I asked the Japanese-American man, Tom, which generation he was. He was *yonsei* (fourth generation). I also asked him how he felt about living in the United States, since he was, according to the report, one-hundred-percent American.

"Of course I feel different. I am Japanese," he said in a soft-spoken manner.

"But you are an American citizen. I have heard that third and fourth-generation Japanese don't think of themselves as Japanese."

"Who told you that?" Tom seemed genuinely surprised. "My face is Japanese. Last year I had my first visit to Japan, and even though I don't speak any Japanese, I felt at ease there."

"Do you have many American friends?" I asked.

"Yes, I have American friends. But most of the time we associate with each other." I knew by "each other" that Tom meant with other Japanese.

"How do you feel when you are with Russell?" I continued. "He is a white American."

"He's great," Tom answered. The two women laughed and the one next to Russell put her arm around his neck—a gesture most orientals would be unlikely to use.

"I like Japanese women. They're cute," Russell teased.

"We have white and black friends," Tom said, in the reserved manner typical of a Japanese man, "but we feel closer among ourselves."

I, too, had found this true. I made many American friends who were very helpful and friendly to me, but I didn't feel comfortable saying to them the things I could say to even my casual Chinese acquaintances. There seemed to be a gap, a lack of a common understanding that is difficult to describe.

At Dr. Liu's picnic, I met Dr. Chou and his Cantonese wife. I had a long talk with Dr. Chou, and since he was from Beijing, this brought us closer. He was older than Dr. Liu and had a Ph.D. in history from an American university.

"We were a bunch of poor students when we came in 1946," Dr. Chou began. "We lived in the cheapest places. We didn't speak much English and didn't know how to cook. We didn't even know what hamburgers or hot dogs were. We once went to a restaurant, ordered hot dogs, didn't like them, and left them on the table. After a while, we learned to cook.

"I studied history because that was the easiest subject for me," Dr. Chou continued. "I got my Ph.D. in 1950. I couldn't go back to China then, after the Kuomintang retreated to Taiwan, and there was no place for me in Taiwan either. I had to find work in the United States. At that time, Americans thought every Chinese was either a laundryman or a cook. They certainly didn't want an oriental to teach their children history. I couldn't find a job. Eventually, I met a Chinese businessman who came from the mainland to the United States after 1949 when the Chinese Communists established a new government in China." Mainlanders refer to this event as "Liberation," and Taiwanese refer to it as the "fall." Chinese in the United States try to avoid using either term, as a compromise.

"This man had brought tens of thousands of dollars with him and established a wholesale business in Chinese goods. I worked for him as a salesman. Later I had my own business as a dealer in Chinese jade and antiques. I am semi-retired now.

"Three years ago I entertained several mainlanders here. I invited many Americans to my home to talk to them. They don't think of Chinese only as laundrymen and cooks anymore."

After the picnic, Dr. Chou invited me, the two women from Taiwan and a few others to his house in Skokie. His living room reminded me of the guest hall for a Chinese wealthy family of fifty years ago: carved hardwood chairs and tables, palace lanterns, scroll paintings, vases of dark green and gold designs, and jade articles. Dr. Chou's wife served us Chinese peanut candies. I saw a bottle of Fengjiu, a famous brand of Chinese spirits, and asked to have a sip.

Lin, the graduate from Taiwan, laughed at me, saying, "You behave like an American, demanding a drink." I remembered the Christmas parties I had attended with the McKnights in December 1980, shortly after I had come to the United States. At that time I dared not take a drink or anything from the buffet table without an invitation from the host. At the Christmas parties one year later, the first thing I did was to get a drink from the bar, with or without an invitation. The shyness, the Chinese table manners, were now gone.

But I was still Chinese enough to be pleased when Dr. Chou told his wife to bring some cold meat to me. It is an old custom for Chinese to serve wine and cold meat to their guests.

The strong spirits tasted sharp and pungent. For so long I had been without my daily habit of a cup of strong liquor and I had nearly forgotten the delicious feeling of spirits trickling down my throat. How many times during those seventeen months I had longed for a cup of Chinese liquor and a piece of Beijing sausage.

I readily acepted Dr. Chou's invitation for dinner a week later, savoring the thought of that bottle of Fengjiu spirits and a dish of cold meat. I was beginning to long for the tastes and smells of home.

CHAPTER SIXTEEN

THE KNOXVILLE WORLD'S FAIR

By the summer of 1982 I had become very close to the people at China Books. I loved the intimate atmosphere and never saw the usual employer-employee relationship there. "You are running a socialist enterprise," I joked with them. They were as polite as Chinese. All four of the employees preferred to work in this small bookstore, even though they had college degrees and could have had better paying jobs. Pam, the manager, had been a college instructor. With their considerable knowledge, these four knew quite a bit more about the books they sold than their Chinese counterparts.

In America I had met a cab driver with an art degree, a man with a doctorate who ran a restaurant, and store clerks with master's degrees. China does not have this surplus of college-educated people; we have to fill many jobs with less-educated people. The job I held called for a university degree, yet I had never been to college. Would the day ever come when we Chinese might let four college-educated people sell books?

I enjoyed these people at China Books and was eager to do

things for them. Back in May, Pam had asked me to go with her for a few days to help set up a book counter in the Chinese pavilion at the 1982 World's Fair in Knoxville, Tennessee. I readily agreed, and later went back there again to spend part of July and most of August.

On my first trip to Knoxville, on May 15, Pam and I loaded up her car and drove off in the afternoon heat. The sights south of Chicago along Highway 94 were familiar to me, since I had passed through the industrial area several times, the gigantic steel mills always attracting my attention.

While we were driving through Gary, a steel town south of Chicago, Pam and I talked about trade unions. Pam's father was a union organizer. I told her that my impression about American unions from the American news media was not so good. In China, we consider the working class as the most advanced class. American workers appeared to be less politically advanced; union members were too small in number, and couldn't play an important role in politics. My journalist and professor friends, perhaps, were more progressive than the factory workers. Pam didn't agree with me: "There are conservative trade unions and bad union leaders," she said, "but there are still progressive grassroots union organizations struggling for benefits for the working class."

It was getting humid and stuffy as we drove south across the flat fields of the Illinois and Indiana plains. I had gotten used to seeing the rich farmlands of the Midwest, and they no longer held much appeal for me. I tried to keep my eyes open so as not to let Pam think I took her driving for granted.

Around eight o'clock we found a hotel on the outskirts of Indianapolis. Each of the two rooms we rented cost twenty-five dollars. Pam told me it would cost forty-five dollars for one room in the Holiday Inn, next to our hotel. Why, I thought, do American tourists complain so much about the cost of Chinese hotels? Our's are much cheaper.

The next morning at six we started out again in the fresh

clean air. The hilly terrain became more and more attractive. For eight hours we drove through the wooded hills of Kentucky and Tennessee. When Pam and I became tired of talking, she played a tape of reggae music and interpreted it for me. I liked it because of its simple rhythms and profound ideas. "Now you got what you want, but you want more," sang Bob Marley. How true that is! People always want more and more.

I looked out toward the valleys beyond the ridge where the highway ran. Occasionally I saw roughly built cabins on the hillsides, each with a small vegetable plot. "The people living in these hills don't make much money," Pam said, "but they love to be away from city masses and noise." I, too, loved to be away from the crowds.

At Knoxville, Mary Ewing, an active member of the U.S.-China Friendship Association, put us up for the first night in her house overlooking the Tennessee River. Early next morning, while everyone was still asleep, I slipped out of the house and walked down to the river. Fish were jumping up through the misty water surface, dead logs floated down the mucky stream, rabbits munched under bushes, and a deer grazed gracefully on the bank on the other side. Looking up and down the river, I wondered why Americans spend thousands of dollars to travel to other countries for a vacation. The scenery along the Tennessee River is at least as beautiful as that along the Li River, the legendary scenic spot in southern China. The difference is that such places in the United States have been changed little by human beings, while the places of natural beauty in China are decorated with artificial creations that represent three thousand years of history. I prefer the unaffected places.

The next day I moved in with the Chinese delegation. Although I had learned, after one and a half years in the United States, to feel at ease in American homes, I still felt more relaxed with Chinese. The days were so busy for Pam and myself, setting up the booth and selling books from

China, that I didn't find time to visit the Great Smoky Mountains, as I had planned. The stream of visitors at the exhibit were mostly from small or medium-sized towns and rural areas in Kentucky, Tennessee, Missouri, and West Virginia. I felt good when I was able to recognize, by one visitor's accent, that he came from St. Louis. They were all very friendly, but not as well-informed about the outside world as were the people in Chicago. My experience there persuaded me that, although American society is quite mobile and has a highly developed communications system, there remain distinct differences between people from provincial areas and those from big cities.

The Chinese Pavilion was the best part of the whole fair; many visitors had to wait outside the gate for two hours to get in. The pavilion contained a dozen bricks from the Great Wall, stone horses excavated from the First Emperor's tomb, as well as Chinese artists displaying their crafts. The staff of forty-two Chinese included: an accountant, a cook, an electrician, a carpenter, a woman embroiderer, a traditional Chinese painter, a painter decorating the insides of snuff bottles, a sculptor carving out pictures on porcelain plates, and four interpreters who had to run about through the exhibits all day in order to translate for the hoards of visitors. They loved the children's books we sold in the pavilion. China has very talented artists who design and draw picture books for children. Such books didn't sell well in Chicago, but people here bought them as souvenirs. Hundreds of handcrafted articles were for sale. The Chinese love machine-made, electronic things; Americans love handmade things. No wonder so few people were interested in seeing the energy-saving devices displayed at the Canadian Pavilion.

For all the Chinese staff, except the delegation head, it was their first time abroad. "Everyone was eager to come to the United States," the electrician told me. "After two months, we now all complain about being tired and bored.

Every day we start work at 9:30 in the morning and finish at 10:30 at night. We are exhausted." The Chinese Pavilion was badly understaffed for such a large exhibit. The delegation head complained of the shortage of people who knew enough English to carry on business.

"Do you have rest days?" I asked the electrician.

"Yes. We take one day off a week in turn."

"Then you can go into town," I said.

"What for? We have very little money to spend; we are not interested in seeing streets and high buildings on an empty pocket. Besides, we have no car to drive there."

China is short of foreign currency and can't afford to pay much to Chinese who go to work in a foreign country. We have to use the money for importing equipment, technology, and grain to feed our people. I knew of the financial plight of the Chinese at the pavilion, and had brought along my camera and three rolls of film to take pictures for them. I didn't have much money either, but compared to them I was much better off on the $400 a month living allowance paid to me by the Chinese embassy.

The delegation head told me that only eight or nine of the forty-two Chinese could speak enough English to communicate with Americans. "It's very difficult," he said, shaking his head. "Those who don't know English can do little but sit behind a counter." Actually, they did a lot. Although they couldn't speak to Americans, they could observe a country and a people alien to them. We Chinese have a lot to learn about the outside world after so many years of isolation.

"We depend on the overseas Chinese too much," the accountant said. "All our negotiations with Americans are done through them. We know no one here, and we know little about the local situation."

The electrician told me that the Chinese staff members didn't like the overseas Chinese merchant who had procured the right for himself to have five or six shops within the Chinese Pavilion. "We set up the show window to attract visitors and now he is making all the money," the electrician said indignantly. In one of his shops I saw products made in Taiwan and Hong Kong, and even some with Japanese trademarks. He had the most profitable part of the Chinese exhibition—no wonder his subordinates had flown to Beijing several times to persuade the Chinese government to send a delegation to the World's Fair. A Chinese-American visitor asked me if the workers in the restaurant run by this overseas Chinese-American merchant were from China. "The food is not good," he said. "And the price is too high." I smiled. I didn't know how to answer the visitor's question; the restaurant employees were damaging China's reputation for fine cuisine.

"Americans are more straightforward in business than the overseas Chinese," a young Chinese worker complained. We were waiting impatiently at ten o'clock in the evening for the Chinese-Americans to close their section so we could all have dinner. "They think only of money." I told him not all Americans are straightforward. My experience had shown me that some of them can be very greedy and crooked. "They try to make money by any means," I said. "Fortunately, we don't have many such people in China today. But the main point is that we should have our own people working here at the fair, and not overseas Chinese."

In 1978, with the help of two Americans, China had sent an exhibition to San Francisco, Chicago, and New York, all a financial disaster. Fortunately, the American public blamed the two Americans for this failure. This time, the Chinese had relied on Chinese-Americans. It had seemed like a good idea, but the bulk of the profits went to the Chinese-American merchant. Mainland Chinese have yet to learn how to do business in the western countries.

On Saturday afternoon, the senior interpreter and the electrician informed me that the kitchen was going to serve a special dinner that evening—beer and wine and several good dishes. I had planned to stay at Mary Ewing's house that night so that Pam could drive me to the airport to catch a plane back to Chicago early next morning. But I didn't want to miss this dinner—the Chinese cook was very good.

I thought I had found a solution. "Could I bring Pam with me?" I asked. "She could have dinner with us and sleep in the women's quarters."

My suggestion shocked the interpreter. "You want to bring an American to eat with us? And sleep in our rooms? How can that be possible? We don't even let overseas Chinese enter our rooms. The delegation head entertains Americans in the guest house with specially prepared food. For two months, there have been no Americans or overseas Chinese in our kitchen and dormitories."

Perhaps I had been in the United States too long to remember how we treated our foreign colleagues in my office. We always thought of our living places as being too shabby for Americans to see. When we did entertain American guests in our homes, we spent half a month's salary to buy the food, so we seldom invited them.

"Our rooms are too messy," the electrician said with genuine concern. "Our food is not good for Americans. Americans don't eat many of the things we eat."

I laughed. "That is not true," I said. "Many Americans love Chinese food. Six of us Chinese rent a house in Chicago. Our place is untidy and we lack furniture, but we entertain professors, doctors, and Chinese-Americans. We cook all the dishes ourselves. You have an excellent cook—the food I eat in your kitchen is the best food I have had since I came to the United States. The food in Chinese restaurants in Chicago is not as good as your's. The place you are staying in is much better than most American homes—definitely much better than our's."

The interpreter, a woman who worked for the Foreign Trade Institute as an English teacher, then told me this story: their bus driver, a local Chinese-American, wanted to stay with them for dinner one night. "I haven't had a real Chinese dinner for a long time," he told them. "I will eat in your kitchen tonight. I'll ask my girlfriend, too." So saying, the bus driver picked up the phone and started to dial. The interpreter translated what the driver had said to the accountant. "No, no, no..." The accountant said, shaking his head and looking panicked. "We don't entertain guests without preparation."

Although the young Chinese-American driver didn't understand Chinese, he did understand the expression on the Chinese faces. His face flushed. Putting down the phone, he said, "I was kidding. I'm sorry." He left. The interpreter had asked the accountant why they couldn't let him eat with the Chinese. "Can't you see how shabby our kitchen is?" the accountant replied.

When I told the interpreter that I often stayed overnight in Americans' homes, she envied me. I said that if I were not allowed to enter Americans' homes, how could I learn about their life? I also told these mainland Chinese that not every American has a car, that not many Americans live in places as elegant as the Beijing Hotel, and that many Americans don't feel comfortable being treated as millionaires when they tour China. They want to be treated like ordinary people. Certainly Americans live much better than Chinese, but not as extravagantly as many Chinese think.

We Chinese should not be ashamed of the fact that China is poor. We can be proud that we are hardworking, intelligent people and we need not conceal our poverty from foreigners. I told the interpreter that when I first came to the United States, I felt embarrassed about the degree of poverty in China. I was even self-conscious about my poor-quality clothes, but when I saw some of my affluent friends wearing casual clothes, I stopped worrying. I had learned that Americans don't laugh at our lack of material things, although a few eccentrics may ridicule us for other reasons. No one ever kept me from talking to or visiting any American family. Instead, many people wanted to make friends with me because I came from China—which they found quite fascinating. They wanted to know about China and her people and their interest made it easier for me to understand them as well.

That night, however, I did not stay for dinner. Instead, I went with Pam to Mary Ewing's so that I could get to the airport on time for my departure. I had been in Knoxville for only four days.

●   ●   ●

When I returned again in July at Pam's request, to spend a number of weeks running the China Books booth, I was glad to get away from the sultry heat of Chicago. This time, I stayed in a dormitory at Tennessee University in Knoxville, and the dormitory and exhibition halls of the World's Fair were air-conditioned.

On this longer trip I was able to explore Knoxville, a medium-sized city built on low hills covered with lush, green trees and grass. The Tennessee River runs under highway bridges and its banks are still hardly touched by man. It is a beautiful city, but what I liked most about it was its quietness. There were no crowds except inside the World's Fair grounds. On my one vacation day out of the whole month while I was in Knoxville, I went to the Great Smoky Mountains and enjoyed the Indian reservation exhibition. When I was staying in the forests of northern Wisconsin, or driving through the national parks of Kentucky, or whenever I was away from the crowded and sprawling city of Chicago, I envied Americans and wished China had such vast stretches of unspoiled land.

●   ●   ●

The theme of the World's Fair was energy conservation, and most countries followed the theme closely. I looked briefly into the Canadian, Australian, and American pavilions; only the gigantic film screen in the American Pavilion

188

seemed worth the time. I didn't bother to see the mummies in the Peruvian Pavilion or the stones from the pyramids in the Egyptian Pavilion. I preferred to spend my time talking to Americans.

Every day I talked to at least a hundred people, answering a thousand questions and asking scores of my own. The people visiting the fair had little knowledge of China. Not many Americans, I soon found out, are interested in what is happening in faraway places. Many asked me where Beijing was, where the Great Wall begins and ends, how Chinese eat with chopsticks (because the gift shop was selling them), and if it were true that all Chinese look alike. A few who were planning to visit China asked me about places they wanted to see. The knowledge I had obtained working as a journalist helped me to answer these questions.

Like the other Chinese at the fair, I went to the Chinese Pavilion at ten o'clock every morning and returned to my room at ten o'clock at night. The days were tiring, but I was happy because I was learning a lot. I could feel my spoken English becoming more fluent with every passing day. I was making much greater progress than I would have if I had stayed in Chicago.

When I became tired of standing at the book counter, I would sit at a table where a Chinese woman sold Chinese stamps. She suggested that I watch how the parents reacted when children chose stamps. "The adults never interfere," she said. "If they agree to buy stamps, they just let the children choose on their own. They don't even give opinions. They only pay for them." At the bookstand I later observed that children had just as much freedom in selecting books. The parents interfered with their children's choices only when a parent didn't want to pay for the selected volume.

Most Chinese parents help their children select purchases. They love their children as much as any parent does, and they like to buy things for them. After a Chinese

189

mother has agreed to pay for an item, she lets her child make a choice. Then she says, "This one is no good," or "That one is better than this one." If the child insists on the one he or she has chosen and it is not to the liking of the mother, more often than not the mother will refuse to buy the thing at all. Those mothers who give too much independence to their children are not considered good mothers by Chinese standards. "She spoils her son too much," her neighbor or colleagues will say.

I like the way American parents treat their children. The young ones are treated as small adults—that's why, I think, Americans are so much more independent than Chinese. In Chicago, I had noticed that parents often left their young children with baby-sitters while they went to a party or to the theater. Chinese parents seldom do that. I made a mental note that, after I got back to China, I would give my son more freedom in deciding his own affairs. My wife is too dominating in this respect. I would persuade her to follow American parental practices.

At the World's Fair many people wanted their names written in Chinese on slips of paper. They paid a dollar for this. At our bookstand we sold Chinese bookmarks, also for a dollar. These were very beautiful bookmarks with either hand-painted miniatures on them or dyed feathers glued on to make pictures. If the purchasers wanted us to write in Chinese on them—their names or whatever they thought of— they paid twenty cents extra. A Chinese-American stood at the counter for five minutes looking at the bookmarks. "You are very smart at making money," she remarked, as she was about to leave. "They are too expensive."

I flared up, but refrained from shouting at her. Certainly in China it would be too expensive to buy a bookmark for $1.00, and no one would want to buy it for such a price, much less spend twenty cents more to have something written on it that they couldn't even read. But one such bookmark requires at least half an hour of labor. In Chicago, the legal minimum wage was $3.75 an hour. Why should we Chinese receive less? This woman, who must have visited China in recent years and seen the low price charged for bookmarks there, was saying to me that our price was too high. I was indignant; yet, at the same time, I felt sorry for us Chinese. We were considered cheap labor.

For three days, a young woman from China sold Qing Dynasty copper coins and stamps at the booth run by the Chinese-Americans, next to our bookstand. One day when she had no customers, she picked up a children's picture book from the bookstand. As she started to look at it, one of her bosses, a middle-aged Chinese-American woman, came over and snatched the book from her hands. "How dare you read books when you do business," the elder woman hissed. "If you don't want to work here, you can leave." It was very humiliating to the young Chinese woman, who had grown up in a society where no bosses dare treat subordinates roughly. The girl choked down her tears as she stood there respectfully.

I was angered by the scene and wanted to embarrass the older woman by saying that she had damaged my book when she snatched it from the clerk's hands and should pay for it. I didn't say anything, but she noticed my look. Several Americans watched the two women, bewildered, but since they had been talking in Chinese, the Americans didn't understand. The young woman, from Shandong Province, had been in the United States for only a year. Since she had to spend much of her after-school time working, she hadn't been able to learn much English. I later comforted her. "You are here to learn," I said. "Keep that in mind all the time. Don't be bothered by people like that insensitive woman. Learn what you can and take it back to China."

This young woman had come to America as many do, believing in the myth that this country has a good life waiting for anyone who dares to come. She didn't have any financial backing and had to make a living while trying to

191

go to college. Comparatively speaking, living in the United States is still easier than living in China, but the plight of such Chinese students in American universities is not enviable. Either because of their vanity or because they wish to save their parents from worry, they don't write home about such things as how many hours a day they spend washing dishes in a restaurant.

At 10:00 every night the tired Chinese workers at the World's Fair exhibit boarded a bus that took them twenty miles to their living quarters in the suburbs. Their place had become crowded and that was why I couldn't stay with them. I would say goodnight to them and walk away alone, showing them how free I was to deal with American life, while they were required to move around in groups. I would walk south through the fair, past the carnival, feeling the excitement of the cheerful crowd—Americans express their emotions very openly. The streets were desolate immediately beyond the World's Fair grounds.

It took twenty minutes to walk from the Chinese Pavilion to my dormitory. I usually walked hurriedly, but one night when I felt sweat on my back from the late August heat, I slowed down. Familiar chirping sounds drifted up from the grass and under bushes, and I stopped to listen to the merry crickets, remembering those early mornings long ago when I had been a naughty schoolboy. In late August I would go with my classmates to catch crickets outside Beijing's city wall, returning just in time for the first morning class, the legs of my trousers and shoes wet with dew. One autumn day my father took me and my brothers out to dig cricket holes in the fields outside Beijing. By now, these fields have been taken over by high-rise buildings.

The dim lights of the athletic center of Tennessee University came into view and a large four-door sedan roared past me. I suddenly remembered that I was in a modern city and not in those rugged vacant lots of my childhood days. Behind me I heard the booms of fireworks that were shot off at 10:30 every night from the fair grounds.

I hurried back to my room, to get a good night's sleep. Tomorrow was another day of the fair—in these last few remaining weeks of my American stay.

CHAPTER SEVENTEEN

TIME TO GO HOME

ome now meant much more than just my wife and our son. It also meant the life I was born into, the surroundings and environment that looked Chinese, the people with whom I shared a culture, and the job at my office which I had, in the past, sometimes resented. I longed for them all. As one Chinese saying goes, all water returns to the sea; all leaves go back to their roots. My roots were in China, in Beijing, in my family. It was time I went home.

Late in August I returned to Chicago from Knoxville. I was tired, physically and mentally. The urge to speak English was gone, and staying alone was becoming unbearable. I told the other visiting scholars about my plans to go home two and a half months early, in September.

"It seems to us you have been the happiest person among us," they said. "You have so many American friends you visit; you go to parties nearly every week. If you can't remain for two years, how can we?" They were scientific researchers, with fewer opportunities to make contacts with Americans. They went only to places which were along the way between their quarters and laboratories, and occasionally on weekends to one or another of the city's shopping centers. They were content with good results in their research or in writing a successful paper, unlike me with my goal of learning all I could about this country through the people.

By now the parties and gatherings I went to began to remind me of my friends in Beijing. In China, when we get together, we talk about the people we know; we gossip and pass on rumors. This small talk, I think, brings people closer—no one has to go out of his way to be especially nice or polite. I couldn't possibly gossip at my American friends' parties. Instead, I dutifully answered their questions to satisfy some of their curiosity. I found that now a dinner in Chicago usually led me to think longingly of supper at home.

In late June I had written a report to the Chinese embassy, telling them I had accomplished my goals in the United States and that I would be ready to go home in September. They sent me a plane ticket for September 11. Much like a string on a bow, I had been taut for twenty months, looking for every chance to speak English, to listen to English, and to go to American places. I therefore decided that now, before I went home, I should relax and loosen up a bit.

I asked Liang, one of my roommates, who was studying computer science, to go with me for walks after supper. It was pleasant to be out in the open in the warm Chicago evenings. We walked south across Taylor Street, through a quiet neighborhood inhabited by Italians and an increasing number of Mexicans; then we turned east to walk around the Juvenile Detention Center. We waved to youngsters on the third floor who would tap at the window glass when they saw us. I had sympathy for them because of their loneliness. We came back along side streets to avoid the foul smell of heavy auto exhaust on Damen Avenue.

"My office is happy with the progress I have been making

here and asked me if I wanted to stay another year or two," Liang told me one night. "But I don't think I will. Two years are enough."

Then, as on every night, our conversation turned to life in the United States. "Yes," Liang would say, "Americans live much better than we do. I have seen how rich people live, with their good clothes, big cars and expensive houses. So what! If their neighbors have a new car, then they want a new one also. They save to buy a house in the suburbs, then find it lonely after they move there. I am not comfortable here and feel I am looked down upon. If I didn't need to learn something from American scientists, I wouldn't stay.

"Naturally, I would like to have the things Americans have, but I want them in China, not here. In four months here I can save as much money as an entire year's salary in Beijing; already I have saved enough to buy a color TV set," Liang continued. "My wife wrote me that her office is allocating new apartments; I hope we will get one and can move soon. My family is still living in a single room of sixteen square yards. My children fight over who will use my desk at homework time. But I know I will never have a house like my Chinese professor has in Chicago; China does not have that much space for everyone."

I reflected on the fact that most of the successful Chinese I had met in Chicago—doctors and professors—never thought of themselves as Americans. "China is my country. Someday I will go back," one professor told me. These Chinese have a deeper sense of homeland than members of other ethnic groups I met in the United States. They have preserved more ancient Chinese customs and traditions than have the Chinese on either the mainland or Taiwan. It appears easier for a European immigrant to adjust to American society; a Chinese always thinks of his homeland. It is not merely a difference of skin color; it is cultural. I was glad to have become more aware of the importance of upholding my cultural values.

After twenty months of observing American life, I had become more satisfied with the idea of my simple life in China, and I hoped that our country would never be one in which money is of first importance. I would never in my lifetime have the many possessions my middle-class American friends have. Yet, it seemd to me as if they were really only living the same cycle of life that I do in China, except on a higher economic rung of the ladder. We shared the same fundamental needs: family, friends, a familiar culture.

• • •

With only a week left, it was time to think about saying my goodbys, packing up my belongings, and finishing my shopping. I had already bought a TV set, a camera, a stereo, and a typewriter for myself. But since I hated shopping, I had not yet bought presents to take back to my family and friends in Beijing. Two of my friends offered to drive me around to the stores, so that I would find the chore less irritating. It took a large part of two days to find the right things to bring home to Beijing.

My friends held farewell parties for me, which I didn't really want to attend; I only wanted to stay home and wait for the day when I would go home. My roommates were in school during the day and I was alone in the house. To keep active I packed, unpacked, and repacked my suitcases. I turned on the television but the programs no longer interested me, so I turned it off. I spent most of the time daydreaming and planning what to say and what to do after I got back home.

Certainly I would not wear my western suit at home, and I would cut my hair short again. In the United States I had tried to dress as Americans do so that I wouldn't stand out. For the same reason, I would dress in my old clothes at home. I would leave the pair of blue jeans behind. I detest those who come back to China from a trip abroad in a shirt, tie, and three-piece suit, often with a camera slung over their shoulder. I think they really only want to show off to other Chinese how important they are.

My relatives probably thought I ate bread and butter all the time, as many returned Chinese have bragged that they did. Butter-and-bread is a phrase implying all western food. I would tell them that most of the time we cooked Chinese food; I wouldn't tell them I had been to restaurants representing seven or eight different kinds of ethnic foods. I would tell them that the United States is still a rich country with abundant natural resources: the coal deposits in Illinois have barely been touched; many areas are covered by forests that would have been turned to farmland in China hundreds of years ago. But I would also tell them the economic situation is not all good. Companies are going out of business; prices are rising; cars in the streets are becoming older and smaller; and unemployment is high at 10 percent. Several Americans I knew had lost their jobs.

Should I tell my relatives that I didn't like the superior or condescending manners some Americans showed me, consciously or unconsciously? Would I say that this was the major reason I sometimes felt uncomfortable in America?

I would have to remember to correct some of the impressions I had created by things I wrote in my first few months here about Chicago's poor black neighborhoods. I had told them about some of the things I had learned from the news media—robberies, killings, and drug sales in the black communities. I said that some of my Chinese friends in America had developed a fear of poor black neighborhoods and, if possible, avoided being near them. I had a better understanding of the black issue now.

I realized that many black families didn't have the opportunities for acquiring good jobs or a good education. I had seen the rundown schools in the poor black sections of Chicago, and had compared them to schools in Chicago's mostly white northern suburbs which had good equipment, even computers, for the students. I knew that quite a few of the Chinese-Americans who lived in expensive

198

neighborhoods did so only because the schools in these neighborhoods were of better quality.

The attitude of the blacks reminded me of my experience with young peasants and children of peasants I met in the outskirts of Beijing when I was assigned the job of looking after the swimming pool my office had there. The young peasants were ignorant and harsh in their manners. They didn't want to pay the required entry fee to the pool, and they constantly fought among themselves, causing fear among the children of the office workers. We who were the temporary guards for the summer didn't know how to deal with them. We wanted to organize a group of workers to block their entry so that they would no longer come to the pool. We never carried out our plan because of an earthquake that permanently closed down the office swimming pool. From that experience I learned to avoid the uneducated youth from villages outside Beijing.

I saw in the black unemployed youth in Chicago the same kind of resentment—a grudge against society—that I had seen in the young men in Beijing who had been deprived of a chance to go to school by the effects of the Cultural Revolution and subsequently could not get jobs. They felt wronged by society, and they could find no one on whom to vent their anger and frustration; they nurtured a hatred for society as a whole. They did not have a cat in their kitchen to kick, so they kicked garbage cans or the public telephone booths; they broke young trees and picked quarrels for no reason. I recognized some of this same hostility in the poor sections of Chicago.

• • •

On September 7 I flew from Chicago to San Francisco. The air was as dry in San Francisco as it is in Beijing at that time of the year. The people at the home office of China Books welcomed me and gave me a tour of the city. Friends in Chicago had told me that I must see Muir Woods near San Francisco, a park where giant redwood trees grow, and I wanted to see the Golden Gate Bridge. The next day Henry Noyes, the founder of China Books, a man over seventy and now retired, drove me to Muir Woods over the Golden Gate Bridge. I was not so impressed by the lofty redwood trees, but the bridge was awe-inspiring. Henry accompanied me on a walk of its full length. I marveled at this great project of steel built more than forty years ago. Several hundred people had jumped off this bridge to their deaths, Henry told me. I found one thing particularly interesting: the temperature varies by at least five degrees from one end of the bridge to the other. I also wondered what had happened to the proposal of a small boy who, a dozen years ago, donated his candy money and suggested that the bridge be painted gold, as its name suggests; the bridge remains red, so perhaps he didn't get much support.

In Chicago everyone told me I should see *ET*, a highly popular science-fiction film. The general manager of China Books, Chris Noyes, and his family, took me to see it on the last night I was in the United States. I liked *ET* for a reason that most American kids might not think of: ET wanted to go home. He couldn't survive on earth, living with his new friends; he wanted to return to his own kind. The film didn't say anything about the planet ET lived on; we don't know if the planet had cars, refrigerators, color TV sets, or divorced parents. The film did show how excited ET was after he had "phoned home" and learned that his people were coming to take him home.

During my stay in the United States I had met many people, some of whom had become very good friends. Many of them were like ET's young friends; they had helped me in every way they could to understand American life. But few of them really understood me or knew why I couldn't feel comfortable among Americans, why I preferred to live a poorer and simpler life in China.

On September 11, 1982, after having spent twenty-one months and thirteen days in the United States, I stepped on the CAAC plane that would take me over the Pacific Ocean to my home. We flew continuously toward the sunset for ten hours; darkness came only after the plane was over China's territory.

I pressed my face against the edge of the window and looked toward the darkened earth. The huge wing of the plane blocked most of my view. Occasionally, an isolated blur of lights twinkled somewhere below and I wondered what place that might be. Ten minutes to ten, Beijing time, a woman's voice announced, first in Chinese and then in English, that the plane was approaching Beijing. Very soon I saw a dim glow over a large area to the left of the plane. I guessed this must be Beijing. I had seen Chicago from the air at night, and felt strangely let down by the fact that Beijing was not as bright as Chicago. To my mind, this city, the capital of a country with a billion people, should have stronger lights than any city in the world.

As the plane descended, individual lights became more and more distinguishable. I strained my eyes trying to see familiar spots, but I couldn't even make out Changan Avenue, the major thoroughfare. The plane banked. Bright-colored ground lights shimmered below us. Who would be there to meet me, I wondered. I had asked Fengyun in a letter not to let people from my office come. I didn't want a conspicuous homecoming.

And, at last, we landed. More than a hundred people ahead of me waited to get off the plane. I restrained myself from squeezing ahead. While I waited, I imagined how Fengyun might look and what I would say to her. In our letters we had agreed we could only shake hands when we met.

After I stepped into the customs room, it took only a minute before I spotted Fengyun standing outside the glass wall that separates international passengers from those meeting them. When we smiled at each other, I felt the worries, tensions, and anxieties of the past 22 months seeping out of my body. Ze, our son, standing behind Fengyun, smiled at me too, a bit awkwardly. He was whispering into his mother's ear.

"You have gained weight," was Fengyun's first comment to me.

"My plane was delayed in San Francisco for one and a half hours," I replied. The openness and aggressive manner I had learned from Americans vanished immediately as soon as I was among my own people.

Ze felt a bit uneasy with me. Trying to behave like a big boy, he offered to carry one of the suitcases. I told him it was probably too heavy for him. "I can take it," he said, smiling. We each took one corner of the case and put it in the office car. We looked at each other and immediately felt close. He is a good son.

Around 11:00 P.M. we were seated in the office car on our way home. Fengyun put her hand on my leg; I put mine on top of her's. With my son, my younger brother, and the office driver present, we could do no more than that. I asked about various friends. Fengyun told me of four friends, not yet sixty, who had died. Strangely, I linked their deaths with my homecoming. By coming back earlier than I was supposed to, I would have two and a half more months of my lifetime with my family.

There were more buildings along the highway from the airport to the city than there had been before I left. The trees along the roadside were taller. The road was in better condition. The street lights were brighter, but not as bright as those from downtown Chicago to O'Hare airport. But the dimness gave an atmosphere of peace and quiet.

Beijing has never been a city with much nightlife. There is little traffic and few people on the streets after ten o'clock. Now the buildings were dark and the people sleeping. I didn't know exactly where we were, but everything was familiar to me. I was now on the soil of my country and I felt secure with my family beside me. I was able to recognize our fourteen-story apartment building, and as I stepped into the elevator I felt as if I had just come back from my office after working late. We got off on the thirteenth floor and entered our apartment. The furniture was placed exactly as it always was.

Fengyun and I talked long after our son went to sleep. Neither of us said how much we had missed each other, how hard life had been for both of us separated. We talked, instead, about what I ate and what she and our son ate. We talked of who had married, and who had moved into new apartments. She also told me she had promised our son that we could have dinner in a good restaurant after I came back. When we finally went to bed, it was four o'clock in the morning.

For a whole week Fengyun was with me every minute. My second day home we went around our neighborhood, joining the torrential stream of human bodies. Beijing's autumn was still dry and dusty, the sun still clear and warm. In the market, fruits and vegetables were plentiful and cheap. Along the roadside everywhere were mounds of pears, apples, cabbbages, celery, cucumbers and green peppers. I was glad to see so many more things available for purchase than two years ago, and shorter and fewer lines of customers waiting to buy them.

Having gotten used to spending dollars to buy groceries in Chicago, I had to restore my perspective to pennies in Beijing. I bought an armful of cabbage for ten fen (five U.S. cents), a basketful of green peppers for another ten fen. In Chicago three green peppers in a plastic wrapper cost eighty cents. Unfortunately, due to careless handling in transport, many green peppers sold in Beijing were broken. Americans are wiser in handling vegetables. They ship them in cartons.

People were complaining that prices on many items had gone up. After the Cultural Revolution, Beijing residents had become very irritable; a small matter could provoke a big quarrel in the street. The city had a campaign going on "to civilize people's manners and to instruct them to be more polite." The manners of salespersons in stores often were intolerable. I needed a transformer for the stereo I had bought in the United States. Fengyun and I went to look for it in several stores. "We don't have it," the person behind each counter would say, not even bothering to raise his eyes. "Where can I find one?" I would ask politely. "How do I know?" the clerk would retort, still looking at his finger-nails. I didn't feel insulted or angry because I knew that they treated everyone equally.

As before, Fengyun wanted to take walks after supper. I used to resist; now I went with her and enjoyed it. As we walked among the mass of humans one evening I vented my feelings aloud. "Look at all these people—we have too many. How much food and labor are needed to produce just one bite of food for every Chinese in a population of one billion?" I told Fengyun about the great forests in Wisconsin, of the endless national parks along the highways of Indiana, Kentucky, and Tennessee. All of them might make good fields. I told her about the unpicked apples on the Missouri farm, about the tomato plant in the backyard of the China Books store in San Francisco that grew through a hole in the cement-covered ground. The plant came up to my shoulder and bore several dozen tomatoes. It grew well even without cultivation, because the soil there is so natu-rally rich. The land in the United States has been used, at most, for only two hundred years, while China's has been used for three thousand.

On the street one day, I saw a man in his fifties selling very small fish, some only two inches long. He told me he had spent an entire day at a lake outside Beijing and had only caught a meager five pounds. These poor little fish could have grown to at least a foot in length within two years, but they were urgently needed for food right now. In Knoxville, at the World's Fair, in a stream in front of the Chinese Pavilion, foot-long carp by the hundreds swam upstream to feed on the kitchen wastes from a local restaurant. Nobody touched them. Americans could spare such fish, just as the Missouri farmer I visited could spare a few apples.

Perhaps the many months of longing for home influenced my views too much. I looked for the good things that were happening. I saw many new apartment buildings, some completed, some under construction; many of my colleagues were negotiating to move into them. I saw roads being built or widened, trees that had been planted, and plenty of food in the markets. My colleagues still complained about the slowness of China's progress, but I believe China is advancing rapidly. Of course, there are still many problems, not the least of which are incompetent bureaucrats and the lack of consistent policies. In this transitional period it will take time to solve our problems. What is hopeful is that the government has recognized the problems and is doing something about them—albeit, slowly.

I saw that China is trying to catch up with the outside world. A pay telephone was installed in a busy Beijing shopping section a week after I got back. At an exhibition, my brother bought unusual items like spiced salt, something never heard of before in China. The new apartments are being built with spaces for washing machines and refrigerators. Several of my colleagues now have refrigerators. Nearly everyone has a television set.

In the streets I saw many motorcycles. Women are now trying to dress in a sexy way; tightly cut, short vests are in fashion in Beijing. Many young men sport western jackets, some with ties. "Wait until you see how they dress in summer," was Fengyun's comment.

I had come back home to China, remembering it as it had been. But after two years away, I found it to be a different China, a more cosmopolitan China, a China moving toward modernization.